I held the sun in my hands

A Memoir

By

Erika Jacoby

First published by AuthorHouse 06/01/04

ISBN: 1-4184-7020-1 (e-book)
ISBN: 1-4184-3267-9 (Paperback)
ISBN: 1-4184-3266-0 (Dust Jacket)

Library of Congress Control Number: 2004091317

This book is printed on acid free paper.

Printed in the United States of America
Bloomington, IN

ACKNOWLEDGEMENTS

I express my gratitude to my husband, Emil (Uzi), without whose constant support and encouragement the writing of these memoirs would not have become a reality. His patience and love enabled me to overcome my vacillation and doubts about the value of my story. He helped me to stay focused, and he sometimes even pushed me to continue with my work when I became too fatigued.

To our children and grandchildren, I am also grateful. They have always expressed an interest in and enthusiasm about the history of our family and wanted to hear about my experiences during World War II. Their love and support created an even more meaningful relationship for all of us.

I deeply appreciate the editorial help of Lynne Kleeger, who was instrumental in helping me with the technical and grammatical aspect of the memoirs and who stayed with me throughout the many revisions and corrections of the manuscript. I value her faith in me in urging me to see this project through.

Howard Rosenberg contributed his extensive experience in the field of photography.

Linda Martin, an English teacher whom I never met, volunteered to read the manuscript as an "outsider." She provided me with valuable and constructive criticism, and she challenged me to deepen the story to include more of my "persona."

Eva Fogelman, Ph.D., a friend and second-generation survivor, gave me invaluable feedback about the book. I value the encouragement and the supportive comments of Dr. Flo Kinsler, a tireless professional working with Holocaust survivors. I also thank my friends, Pearl Taylor, Monica Rosenberg, Ora Band, and many others who strengthened my desire to write my story and to have it published.

I am indebted to the thousands of young people and adults who sought me out to hear my story and provided me with listening ears and empathic hearts, when most people did not want to hear or know.

DEDICATION

This book is dedicated to my loving family:

To my husband, Emil (Uzi) Jacoby, my sons and their wives, Jonathan and Donna, Benjamin and Etta, Michael and Cary, and my grandchildren, Jesse, Joshua, Shalom Tzvi, Shaina, Doovie, Yaakov, Simcha, Ariel, Ben, and Yael.

To the memory of Anyu, my mother (Malvina Miriam), who survived with me the Holocaust.

To the memory of my father Yakov Koppel (Jeno) and my brother, Moshu (Tibor), and the more than 50 members of my immediate family whose lives were cut short, and to all who suffered and perished in the Holocaust, *"Al Kiddush Hashem."*

TABLE OF CONTENTS

FOREWORD

In her insightful "Afterthoughts" to her remarkable memoirs, Erika Jacoby wonders, as do some Holocaust survivors who have returned to a creative, satisfying life, if she is psychologically healthier than other survivors. This is not a routine query: Jacoby is a clinical social worker who has worked in this field for over three decades and has certainly assisted many other human beings cope with the challenges and traumas of their lives. Here and throughout her narrative, she recounts her experiences with a keen self-consciousness happily free of analytical jargon:

> *I often wonder if I am psychologically healthier than*
> *many other survivors are, and if I am, then I ask myself to what*
> *I owe this. Perhaps it is because my experiences were not as*
> *horrendous as those of other survivors from countries such as*
> *Poland and Czechoslovakia who had spent longer periods in*
> *the camps. Or perhaps it is because I was able to keep my faith*
> *during and after the Holocaust. But the explanation that sounds*
> *most real is that I survived with Anyu, my mother. I knew in*
> *the camps that I would not give up and become a Musulman,*
> *one who lost all will to live, because I had to stay alive for my*

mother. I had to take care of her—I couldn't let her lose another
child.

It is perhaps true that her experiences, as horrible as they were, "were
not as horrendous as those of other survivors." It is true that like other Hungarian
Jews, Erika was not deported until late spring of 1944 and thus had less time
to spend in the camps until her liberation on May 8, 1945. After two periods
in Auschwitz and in Plasow, she was transferred to a smaller camp known as
Wiesau, where the Kommandant was relatively humane, and then to a factory
for aircraft parts in Langenbielau. Factory work during the last months of the
war was certainly less demanding than digging trenches outdoors. She was also
fortunate in having with her throughout, not only her mother, but a young aunt,
cousins, and a few friends from home. Together they could attempt to maintain
some semblance of the religious life they had lived in Miskolc, their home in
Hungary. The descriptions of their sharing an apple for Tu Bishvat, or Erika's
struggle not to eat bread during Passover of 1945, are profoundly moving.

The last explanation of Erika's survival and successful rehabilitation, her
relationship to her mother, is the one that "sounds most real." It is the matrix of
the entire memoir that turns out to be much more than an account of "survival in
Auschwitz." And Erika Jacoby is eminently aware of this crucial, complicated
relationship:

This "duty to stay alive for her" also determined our
relationship in the years following the war, with both positive
and negative consequences. This memoir would not be complete
if I did not look at this relationship that has changed from what it
had been before the war.

Note the adjectives used to describe the mother: strong, independent,
dedicated, devoted, disciplined, brave. Though marginally involved with Erika

before the war, she gave her "a sense of security." "But things changed during the concentration camp and after that. In the camps I discovered that my mother could not save me from all the suffering; indeed, she could no longer take care of herself. I became *her* protector—I saw her as powerless."

What the narrator never says, but the reader can readily assess from the text, is that the daughter is very much her mother's child: strong, devoted, disciplined, brave, and a person of great faith. If one can characterize persons from anecdotes in a narrative, one would say that the daughter is a survivor: she will endure the atrocious conditions of the camps; she will have the will and stamina to survive. The relationship between mother and daughter is not free of tensions even in the camps, and there are several scenes where this surfaces. Among the thousands of memoirs of life in the camps, there are relatively few in which this primal relationship is still at play since there were very few cases in which parents and children were together in a variety of camps. Erika, for instance, had been separated from her father and her brother before she was deported to Auschwitz and learned about their deaths only upon liberation.

For me one of the most moving scenes takes place in Chapter Five when the women prisoners, newly arrived at Auschwitz, were forced to strip in the presence of the German soldiers. We read this passage with full awareness that these are pious women with deep religious feelings about personal modesty.

We were quickly ushered into a large room and told to get undressed. It took a while for me to understand the instructions even though I understood German. It seemed unbelievable that they would ask us to shed all our clothes in front of a swarm of Nazi soldiers and Kapos. I took my clothes off, folded them neatly the way I was taught by my mother, but left my underwear on. The next minute I was hit on my back,

and the Nazi guard yelled: "you take off everything, do you
understand?" I looked around and saw that Anyu was stepping
out of her underwear, and for the first time in my life, I saw her
body completely naked.

This traumatic experience of a 16-year-old girl is told some 60 years
later with a rare combination of clarity and controlled compassion. At the time
of writing, she had already lived through the experiences of the camps and
liberation, migrated with great hardship to the United States, raised a family
of her own, and completed a successful career as a clinical social worker.
And though Anyu had already passed away, she lives in all the fullness of her
character in the memoir of her acutely perceptive daughter.

Arnold J. Band, Ph.D., Professor of Hebrew and Comparative Literature,
UCLA

ॐ

INTRODUCTION

"What is that number on your arm?" asked 11-year-old Danny, sitting under the majestic oak tree in the Hebrew class that I taught at Camp Ramah of California.

His simple question and the earnest expression on his face startled me. Until now very few people wanted to find out anything about my background, and I was just as eager not to bring it up. I wanted to just blend in, not to be noticed for more than what my Zsa Zsa Gabor accent betrayed.

Danny's question aroused the interest of the other kids in the class, and pretty soon we forgot the intricacies of Hebrew grammar and opened up a dialogue, the likes of which I had not experienced until then. They wanted to know about my family and my home; they questioned me about the camps. I told them about Europe, World War II, Hungary and how my life unfolded from the time I was their age. I was aware of their developmental stage—and I was careful not to overwhelm them with frightening information. But they were so eager to hear my stories that they put on their best behavior, and they even did their assignments fast so they could get their reward—the "history" class.

To my surprise, I felt as if I had taken off a heavy coat that had kept me protected from the chilly winds but now had become too burdensome. Suddenly

I felt it was safe to talk about the tragic events of my childhood and youth, that these children would not regard me as some kind of freak or, worse, one who is not telling the truth. On the contrary, they embraced me with their warmth and empathic interest, and that gave me the courage to start on this journey of informing young and old, anyone who wanted to know, to understand, what happened to our people in Europe during those horrible years. From that sunny morning in Ojai, some time in the '60s, to this very day, I have been talking to anyone who wants to know. I go to schools, universities, churches, and synagogues, wherever I am invited to tell those stories. Mostly I want the young people to listen—they are the ones who hold the key to the future.

There weren't many survivors at that time who were willing to expose themselves or risk feeling re-traumatized by reliving their experiences. It took many years until they felt encouraged enough by their fellow Jews, or sometimes non-Jews, or in other cases, by many years of therapy, to open up and start the process of healing. For I am convinced that it was that first storytelling at Camp Ramah that initiated my own slow but continuous recovery. Although I still choke up at certain parts when I speak and am unable to contain my tears, that too is progress: I am not afraid that I will be judged for my "weakness," that I have to hide my emotions the way I did in the beginning when I kept rigid control over my voice and tears.

I get letters after my presentations from the students, who convince me that it is important to go on and talk to them even if sometimes I feel tired and depleted. "My generation must teach our kids what you have taught us, to have respect and be very tolerant of others," writes a bright eighth grader from a Chatsworth, California middle school. "Thank you for opening our eyes to the hate and problems of the world, which we have so blindly ignored," writes Christopher from the same school. Or the letter from perceptive Salmien: "I am not Jewish but I am a Moslem, and I believe that your faith in God helped you to be able to share your story with us and make us realize how much of a tragedy the Holocaust really was." And again, "I will never think that I am better than anybody because we are all equal. I will try my best to stop racism and discrimination."

Another student from a Burbank middle school wrote: "I feel that we are very lucky to live in a free country." And a high school student wrote, "Your speech had a very big impact on all the students. We learned not to take things for granted, and to appreciate the good things in our lives." An 11th grader wrote: "You are doing an amazing service to us by speaking with us, and sharing these details of the Holocaust which fills maybe one page in our history books. We cannot comprehend the horror by reading some numbers on a page." Many students expressed a desire to learn more, and they have even asked me to continue to write to them, sending me their addresses. This book is for them and for all the thousands of students who have gained knowledge and understanding through my story and who, I hope, will carry forward the lessons they learned from it.

And this book is for my children. When our sons were little, they learned some things that other children their age did not. When four-year-old Benjie saw a Volkswagen behind me on the freeway, he would warn me, "Mom, the Germans are after you." He collected and admired little cars but he knew which we would not buy because they were made in Germany. When my mother, Anyu, was especially angry, I calmed the children saying, "She is just upset today because Anyu's family was taken away on this day long ago." Or when she yelled at me for allowing the boys to do something adventurous, I explained to them: "She is too scared that something terrible will happen to you." They seemed to have understood, even forgive her for her bossiness. They never asked where or why—somehow they must have thought that it would hurt me.

And that was an unspoken law in our home, never to cause Anyu, or to my husband, Uzi, or me pain or fear. Of course that meant that we, as parents, didn't know about many of the things our children did, because they were protecting us from the knowledge that would cause us to be worried or frightened. Subconsciously they got locked into their self-imposed separation from us, when, ironically, we wished for just the opposite. They just copied my and Uzi's behavior with my mother, not telling her anything that would upset her, not asserting myself with her because it might cause discomfort. Uzi went along with this; it was important to him to maintain calmness and not to alienate the only living parent we shared. Expressions of anger were discouraged, even perceived as forbidden; only my mother had permission to rage.

And so I wrote this book for our children's children. They are not afraid to ask us "what happened," and they want to know our history and about the lives of our families before and during the war. We welcome these questions and are glad they don't feel constrained by their parents' protectiveness toward us.

Finally, I had to write it all down. I had to see, in black letters on white paper, what filled my head, occupied my thoughts, and often squeezed my heart all these years. I had to take off my heavy coat.

Sometimes I wonder why I need to keep alive this burdensome past. The world has not learned much since then—atrocities, wars, cruelty have not been eliminated. I even wonder sometimes whether the Holocaust has given "permission" for the institution of genocide—permission to disseminate and copy the monstrous barbarism of the Nazi era, by other groups, nations. Even though I am convinced that the Holocaust was a unique, unprecedented event that will mark the 20th century as the most cruel and unforgiving era of human history, and that its lesson must teach humanity to reject barbarism and strive for a moral life, sometimes I want to give up and say: "It's no use!" But I don't, and I go on. If I can influence a single person to fight evil and not to accept prejudice, intolerance, and injustice, I have fulfilled my role. "It is not my duty to finish the work, but it doesn't excuse me from starting it," says the Talmud. So I have written this book as a modest attempt to bring us closer to a saner world.

IN THE BEGINNING — Miskolc

It was a beautiful spring day, May 1st, 1928, Anyu related to me in a letter years later, when she ran out into the street, looking for a midwife to help her deliver her third child. She was sure it would be the girl she longed for. She already had one son who was three years old; a second son would have been 18 months old had he lived longer than a few days. She found Mrs. Weiss, who quickly left her dishes on the table, wiped her hands on her apron, and ran across the street to my mother's kitchen where the water was already boiling in the big pot and white sheets were ready to be torn for use in the delivery. My mother said I came easy and fast, and she was deliriously happy because, indeed, I was a girl. She named me Erika, a name she picked out from a novel just because she liked it. No one else in the community had been given that name, which showed my mother's independent streak. I was also given a Hebrew name, Hava, the name of my father's mother, who had died when my father was a young child. That was the tradition—a newborn was given a Hebrew name of someone in the family who was deceased.

My parents had just opened a kosher restaurant after my father's textile business failed in the depression. My mother always blamed my father for not declaring bankruptcy, like most people had; instead he paid off all his debts, and they remained penniless. It was with my mother's father's help that they started this new venture. He even sent them a woman to cook for the restaurant because Anyu (mother in Hungarian) never learned to cook before she got married; instead she always helped my grandfather in his business, and left the domestic work to her younger sisters and to help my grandmother. Anyu told me that she and my father had a difficult time when they first opened the restaurant; they were always occupied and pre-occupied, and having an active three-year-old boy, they did not have much time or patience for a new infant. They had left my care mostly to the maid: "You just grew up by yourself," she said to me later.

"Put her in the laundry basket on the floor," said Anyu to the maid, Mari. "Even if she turns over, she won't fall far."

So I watched the world from the basket, my eyes following the quick movements of the kitchen staff, and the clatter of pots and pans lulled me to sleep. When I was about a year old, I turned the basket over and started to walk.

"She's a little bit wobbly on her legs yet. That's why she looks like she's limping," said Anyu, while filling the platters with food, which my father took into the restaurant to serve the guests.

"It is best if we send her to my parents in Edeleny for a little while. There my brothers and sisters will take care of her," my mother continued.

"But she is so little," objected Apu (father in Hungarian), at first. But then he agreed. He trusted that my mother knew what was best for me. "Maybe they'll have more time and patience to teach her how to walk straight."

The following week my mother took me on the train to the little village of Edeleny, about 20 kilometers from our city, Miskolc. Edeleny had about five thousand inhabitants, mostly farmers and coal mine workers. The less than one hundred Jewish families got along well with the mostly Catholic population.

I did not learn to walk straight in spite of the urging of my uncles and aunts, and eventually I was shipped back to Miskolc. My father took me to a doctor, who discovered that I had a congenital hip displacement and recommended an operation.

"She is a good candidate for surgery," said Dr. Molnar, a kind, round-faced man whom I instantly liked after he gave me a candy.

"But we know several children who still limp even after the surgery," countered Apu.

"It's true I cannot guarantee that it will be successful, but it's worth a try," Dr. Molnar said in the voice of the expert.

Now it was my father who convinced my mother about the surgery.

"If she were a boy, it would not be so important, but who will marry her if she limps? My own mother suffered all her life with a dislocated hip, but back then they couldn't help her."

I was told that I was two years old when I had surgery on my right hip. Following the surgery, my leg and hip were put in a cast, which stayed on for a year. I spent most of the time on the kitchen table where they could keep an eye on me. Once I fell off the table but did not break anything. The cast was changed a few times when they took X-rays, and Dr. Molnar was pleased with the results. When the cast was finally removed, I still limped, but Dr Molnar assured my parents that it was only a bad habit and eventually I would walk straight.

After the cast was removed, my parents decided again to take me to Edeleny where I could get massage therapy. Mrs. Csiszar was a large peasant woman with strong hands. She came every day with a bowl of some kind of fat which she generously smeared on my body while she kneaded and pushed, pinched and patted my leg for an interminable time, and no begging or crying could save me from her torturous hands. A few times I even hid from her before

3

she came, but someone would always drag me out of my hiding place. When I walked around, my uncles would watch me to see if I walked straight. If I did not, they would threaten me, saying: "Tomorrow they will burn those who limp." Years later, indeed the Nazis did just that. When, as an adult, I had a hip replacement, the nurse remarked that I started to lift my leg immediately after surgery, when I was not fully awake yet, murmuring, "I don't want to be burned."

Miskolc, a midsize Hungarian city where I was born, was in the northeastern corner of the country. There were about 60,000 people living there at that time, a population that consisted of businessmen, factory workers, some professionals, and government workers. There was a Main Street, where most of the businesses were located, and side streets, straight and curved, where people lived, some in single homes but most in apartment buildings. Those who were financially able lived on Main Street in the more expensive apartments.

The Jewish population was counted to be about 10,000, middle class mostly, with a sprinkling of more affluent ones and a good number who could be called poor. The Jews were all members of the "Jewish Community;" that is, they were obligated to pay membership whether they were practicing their religion or not, because only members of the community could be married by a rabbi or buried in the Jewish cemetery. There were two large synagogues: one was called Orthodox and the other Status Quo, which was something like the conservative-reform denomination in the United States. There were also several smaller congregations, one of which was the *Sfardish-Shul*, where my family belonged. This was more traditional than the large synagogue, and the rules and the laws of the Torah were strictly observed. The Shul was catty-cornered from our house, so my father and brothers didn't have to walk far to attend services morning and evening.

A year and a half after I was born, my younger brother, Tibor, or Moshu as we called him from his Hebrew name of Moshe, arrived, so I became a middle child. I often envied my older brother for his privileges as the first-born and my younger brother for being, I believed, my mother's favorite; mostly I envied them both for being boys. They could do more things, were allowed to climb trees or ride a bike, and later, when my older brother Yitzhak was sent to a Yeshiva, I wished that I could do that too. I wanted to explore the mysteries of the Talmud and become a scholar, something a girl could never achieve there. Of course, I did not envy them when they were beaten up on their way to Hebrew school by the Gentile boys, but even that just proved how heroic they were for being able to get away from them.

Our maid, Mari, was the daughter of the cook, Mari neni (Aunt Mari). She came to live with us when she was very young. Although Mari was uneducated, like her mother, she became like an older sister to me. She took me with her everywhere she went, and in turn, I helped her with her tasks around the house. Apu did most of the purchasing for the restaurant, and when he came home with two basketfuls of live chickens, Mari and I took them to the *shohet* (slaughterer) to be killed, according to the ritual law. Then we would sit in the courtyard, plucking chicken feathers all afternoon. She learned the Jewish customs, even the prayers, and sat me down on a little stool at the door to our bedroom and recited the evening prayers with me. Then she sent me to say good night to my parents, who kissed me and turned off the lights.

I was sent to a Jewish nursery school where I was taught German and Hungarian songs and instructed in etiquette. I loved the songs but hated learning the manners—I just did not want to learn how to curtsy or how to close the door politely. My brothers did not have to learn all that, and I envied them for it. But I

5

loved our teacher, "Uncle" Kallos, a sweet, elderly man, who often talked to us in German, and I tried to please him by complying with his instructions.

I was a happy child, benignly neglected by my parents, but I got attention from others, including the guests in our restaurant, and of course, our maids. I looked up to my mother as the one who knew everything, but who had little time or interest in playing with me. She did not believe in having toys either. Later, when my children were growing up, she became very critical of my toy-buying urges. My father had more patience, and sometimes he would say that I was his most beautiful daughter. Of course, I knew that I was his *only* daughter. Still it felt good to hear it, in contrast to my mother who had said repeatedly that I was ugly. She did that, she explained, so that I would not become conceited.

"Tell me a story," I used to plead with Apu as I curled up in his arms on his bed.

"There was once a bee and a wasp," he started. "Shall I tell you more?"

"Yes!" I shrieked with delight, and he repeated, "There was once a bee and a wasp. Shall I tell you more?" On and on he repeated, until I left his bed in frustration.

Shabbat was a special day, because we spent time together as a family. We had our meals with our parents, in contrast to weekdays when we ate by ourselves. I loved walking with my parents on Friday nights, in the winter, the snow making crunching noises under our feet as I tried to measure my steps to Anyu's. In summer on long Saturday afternoons, we would all go to the *Nepkert*, which was a big park with beautiful chestnut trees where all the children played while our parents discussed world events. "Is this good for the Jews?" I would often hear from the grownups, but I did not understand what that meant, just as I didn't understand why on Sundays we would not go to the park, because on that day the Christians had their holiday there and Jews were not to be around then.

There were often conversations about war, anti-Semitism, and the struggle to make a living. But in spite of the adults' conversation, which was often filled with anxiety, I felt I had nothing to worry about. The routine of everyday life gave me a feeling of security, and the little pleasures that came my way must have made me a happy child.

శ్రీ

SCHOOL DAYS

I turned six in May 1934. School started in September, and I couldn't wait. Now I could also learn to read and could show off to my little brother, Moshu, who was almost five, that I was smarter than he, and that Anyu liked me also, even if he had dimples and I didn't. Then two days before classes started, I came down with fever and my skin turned orange-yellow. "Jaundice," said the doctor. "You must keep her home. She can't go to school."

The doctor prescribed some awful medicine that I had to drink every day. Apu stood next to my bed with the tall glass in his hand and instructed me to close my eyes and start drinking without thinking. "*Egyszerre, egyszerre*" he said in Hungarian, meaning that I could not stop drinking, even to take a breath, until it was all finished. I listened to my father, because he never forced me to do anything that was not good for me. He smiled at me with kindness, but I knew that I had to obey him. He stood next to my bed; he looked so tall, his head and face closely shaven. I looked at him while gulping the bitter medicine, and I tried to figure out if his hair was blond or brown, while I drained the glass. Every morning and evening I was wrapped in ice-cold wet towels to bring my fever down, then I stayed in the wet towels until they became warm from my body.

What a relief it was when they were finally taken off, which sometimes didn't happen until hours later because everyone was busy.

I recovered in six weeks, and my mother and I walked to the Israelite Elementary School and met my teacher. Her name was Mrs. Kardos; I immediately disliked her because she would not let me stay in school since everyone had already learned to read.

"Until you catch up, you'd better stay home. I can't teach you separately with 42 other children in the class. Here is the book. When you learn to read, come back."

Anyu took the book in one hand and me in the other, and we walked home. Then she sat me down on the steps in front of the house and said in a no-nonsense voice: "Now you'll learn how to read," and we sat there all day. By the time the evening stars appeared in the sky, I had learned the alphabet and read from the book. The next day Mari walked me to school, book in my hand. I greeted the teacher who sat me in the front row, and instructed me to put my hands behind my back the way all the other children did. I waited to be called by the teacher, eager to show her what I learned, but there were 42 little girls there, and I did not get my turn. I walked home, alone, ate my dinner, and the day was over. My parents were busy in the restaurant and no one asked me how my first day was in school.

Kardos neni (Mrs. Kardos), my teacher, never liked me very well, either. It started when I took to school a mechanical pencil that my grandmother had brought me from one of her trips. I was very proud of my souvenir and was showing it off to my classmates when Mrs. Kardos reprimanded me for distracting the students from their work. To my dismay, when I came back from the play-yard after the ten o'clock break, my pencil was gone—it just disappeared from my desk. I was heartsick, but I saw that the pencil was on the desk of my classmate Vera.

"Give me back my pencil!" I demanded. "It is mine."

"No," she said. "I got it from my father."

"You are lying," and I turned to the teacher. "Have her give me back my pencil. I got it from my grandmother."

Vera denied that she had taken the pencil, and the teacher did not pursue it further. I knew that I would get no help from Mrs. Kardos, so when Vera went to the bathroom, I took the pencil from her desk and hid it in my pocket. She did not cry but told the teacher about it. Mrs. Kardos ignored both of us, and I felt that justice was done. When I got home, I took the pencil out of my pocket and looked at the beautiful picture of the thermal bath on it, where my grandmother had gone to cure her arthritis.

My older brother, Zoli, whom we called Yitzhak, his Hebrew name, was always in trouble. Sometimes he skipped school, and I had to devise an excuse for his absence. His teacher was Mrs. Shebo, a very nice person, who liked me a lot. Mrs. Shebo would often rescue me when my teacher punished me for something, telling Mrs. Kardos that I was not at fault. One day, Mrs. Shebo called me to her room and asked me why my brother was absent the day before. My heart started to pound, my throat got dry, and I felt like I would choke. I knew that I had to lie because my brother had a big *ferheren* (test) in Hebrew School, and he had to study for that, so he skipped school. Somehow neither my brother nor I would dare to tell her the truth, perhaps sensing that Mrs Shebo would not consider Hebrew studies important enough for him to stay out of school. I wanted to say something that was believable, something different that would help my brother, rather than just saying he had a cold.

11

"He had a terrible earache and that's why he stayed home." I looked down, and wanted to run away, but I knew that my brother needed me.

"So, how come he said that he had a cold? Now who is telling the truth?" Mrs. Shebo looked at me, scrutinizing my face.

Oh my God, now I blew it, I thought. Now she will never believe me again, and Yitzhak will get a bad grade. But he was not very interested in his grades, and he did not get upset about the whole incident—only I felt guilty. Mrs. Shebo forgave me and continued to be my ally whenever something came up with my teacher.

I had good friends, and I often played in their homes because they had dolls and I didn't. Anyu never had a real childhood, since she had to help her parents from an early age on and didn't believe in "wasting time" playing with toys. She always urged me to read books instead. Later when I got older she would consider reading so important that she would even forgo asking me to help. I always longed for her approval, and even as an adult I sometimes neglected housework in favor of reading: "The dishes will wait—go ahead and finish that book," she would say. We had only a few books in our home: an encyclopedia of WWI, a book on nature, and a story book about two dogs. The last two books were prizes Anyu received in school for being a good student. I studied these books and also borrowed others from a rich friend who had an extensive library. When I had money, I rented some books from a lending library. Of course, my father had a large collection of Hebrew books, the many volumes of the Talmud and others, and he spent many hours a day in studying them, but I had no advanced Hebrew education so I could not understand those books.

I loved school because there was always something exciting there. I went to school even if I was sick, because it was better than staying home and being bored. The schools, elementary and middle schools, belonged to the Jewish

community where most of the Jewish children went. There were separate schools
for boys and girls. There was also a Jewish Teachers' Seminary for girls where
I planned to go after middle school. I got much recognition for being a good
student, a good athlete, and for getting along with others. Anyu took it for granted
that I always received straight A's, and she seldom came to parents' meetings.
Instead she sent my father, who reported back to her about my achievements.

"It is expected that Erika will do well. She shouldn't be praised for it
because she will become conceited," she would respond. I accepted this without
complaining, but it did hurt when my friend Judy's mother was boasting about
Judy's achievements. It took me many years to believe when someone said
something complimentary, either about my looks or about being smart, that it
could be true.

As a girl, I went to the synagogue only for special services. Later, in
middle school, we had our own Junior Congregation in which I was often the
"cantor" because of my strong voice. Of course, Apu, Yitzhak, and Moshu
attended services not only on Shabbat, but also every morning and every evening.
On the High Holidays, I went with Anyu, and we sat on the second floor where
I had a perfect view of the sky-blue ceiling, and I daydreamed while I watched
the gold stars painted on it. Curtains separated the women from the men below,
but we heard the loud chanting of the prayers. I was awed by the crying, pleading
voice of the rabbi as he uttered the blessings before the blowing of the *Shofar*
on Rosh Hashana. When I looked up at Anyu, I saw tears wet her cheeks as she
blew her nose into her handkerchief. I didn't understand why she was crying, but
I knew that something serious was going on, and that God was deciding whether
we were good or not. I tried hard to cry also but my eyes remained dry. The air
was heavy with sighs, and I could not find comfort in the hard wooden benches,
so I was glad when the service was over and I could run outside.

I was always encouraged to exercise to strengthen my leg following the hip surgery. In the winter I used to go ice-skating with my friends several times a week. One day my parents were called in by the rabbi, who told them that I should not go ice-skating because there were boys at the rink, and it was not a "proper" activity for a religious girl. Anyu became angry and spoke up, telling the rabbi that he should not interfere in this matter. Apu apologized to the rabbi, but was glad that he didn't have to confront him; my mother did it *for* him, again. Whenever there was some kind of conflict, it was usually my mother who would speak up, and not my father. I continued going ice-skating, and I looked at my mother with awe and felt secure because I knew that she would always be courageous for me.

Every summer, because my parents were busy in the restaurant, we children were sent to our grandparents in Edeleny. I loved going there—there was so much more to do, although sometimes I became homesick. My grandfather owned a number of businesses and my many uncles and aunts were in charge of them. They were also in charge of my brothers and me and tried to keep us out of trouble. My youngest uncle, Ali, who was two years older than my brother, was often the instigator, and we followed him blindly. One day, when I was about five, my brother Yitzhak and I went down to the wine cellar and decided to taste the wine in the barrels. They found us there, several hours later, wine flowing freely from the barrels and the two of us passed out on the floor. At another time we sneaked into the grain storage and had great fun "swimming" in the deep mounds of wheat kernels. It took the doctor a long time to clean out all my orifices. When I climbed into the wooden gutter that was part of the bowling alley and it broke under me, my leg got hooked on one of the nails. My aunt Ilonka declared, "That's it! This girl is worse than ten boys. Maybe we'll have to send her home!"

That's what I really wanted, but I panicked that I would be punished; I promised to be good. I was really homesick and wanted to go home, but I was afraid to admit it. Instead, I wrote a letter to Anyu, telling her that my aunts didn't treat me right, that they even hit me, and that I wanted her to come and take me home. I never got an answer to my letter; nor did she come to take me home. I was eight years old, and when I later asked her why she didn't come for me, she said, "I knew that my sisters and brothers would not harm you." And she was right. My Aunt Lilli was always my protector—she took me with her everywhere, even when she met with a boy, a secret I never divulged to anyone. My Aunt Edith had lived with us in Miskolc for many years while she was going to school. She was my idol and my rescuer when I needed help with my homework. To my older aunts and uncles I was usually an irritating pest, but they admonished me with love.

My grandfather, Joseph Salamonovics, was born in Nagyszeretva (Czechoslovakia), cca. 1871. He was a tall handsome man, with a short white beard, always neatly dressed in a dark suit, snow-white shirt and a bow tie. He lost his father at a young age and he quickly became an independent, enterprising young man. He was respected by all, young and old, Jews and Christians. He was the only Jew in the little town who was elected to be a representative in the county government. He was a partner in a coal mine that provided employment to most of the town. When the workers got paid, they got drunk in the tavern, which was also owned by my grandfather, or spent their money in his lumberyard and in my uncle's grocery store. Anyu told me a story that when she was still at home, she used to be in charge of the tavern. Sometimes, late at night, one or another of the peasants would not want to leave and in his drunkenness would yell:

"I'll kill you one day, you rich Jew, and then I won't have to pay back all the money I owe you."

Only my mother was able to calm him down; she was never afraid to talk to any of them, and they would not harm her.

I loved my grandparents, and we grandchildren looked up to them. My grandmother, Julia Horowitz, (Yitel) was a tiny woman, working day and night, but always with a smile. She had severe arthritis, walked with a cane, and would often travel to thermal baths for relief. Even when she was angry or tired, she never raised her voice. The story was told that when my grandfather was ready to get married, he came on horseback to look at her in the village of Mucsony, where she had lived and which was not far from Edeleny, but he passed by her, thinking that she was only a little girl. She was almost 16, and they married a few weeks later and moved to Edeleny. They lived with my grandfather's widowed mother. However, my grandmother did not like how her mother-in-law ordered her around, so one day she left and walked back to her parents' home in Mucsony. It took my grandfather much persuasion to get her to come back after he promised that they would move into their own home. Thus, my grandmother was the first to stand up for women's rights, way back toward the end of the 19th century, in a little village. She came from a very distinguished family, the Horowitz dynasty, with a long line of courageous women and famous rabbis, claiming their ancestry to the 15th century in Prague and in Poland.

I don't remember my grandmother talking very much. It was usually my grandfather who ruled the table at dinnertime, and of course, we children were not allowed to talk at all during the meal. I had to finish everything on my plate, but when I didn't like something, I would secretly give it to the dogs that were always conveniently under the table.

But my grandmother taught me a lot. She showed me how to braid the dough for the Shabbat *chalah* (twisted bread) and how to iron a man's shirt. She felt this was important for me to learn for my future role as a mother and wife. Even after raising twelve children, she never tired of instructing her grandchildren. Around Passover she explained that it was very important to keep a good relationship with the Gentile neighbors, so she carefully packaged some freshly baked *matza* and sent me to their houses with the gift. When Christmas came around, she graciously accepted the special cookies they sent us for the holiday, even though we could not eat them because they were made with lard. We got along well with the Gentile neighbors and they showed respect for us. Only when they had their Easter procession around town were we instructed to stay indoors and pull down the iron shutters to protect our store windows in case they became hostile toward the Jews. My grandfather explained that the Catholic Church blamed the Jews for the crucifixion of Jesus, even though that wasn't true.

My grandfather used to take me to the coal mine with his horse and buggy, which was a special privilege. On the way he would tell me stories from the Torah, always pointing out how God had helped our forefathers and if we were good, he would do the same for us. He used to tell me that when the Messiah comes, there would be bread growing on trees, that we would all roll all the way to the land of Israel, and everybody would be happy. When he took me to the coal mine, he let me loose and went about his business. I explored the area, sometimes getting a ride all the way down the mineshaft, sometimes taking a ride in the cable cars that carried the coal. Later, when my grandfather suffered several strokes and could no longer talk or walk alone, he would just sit in his chair and stare into the air. I felt so helpless. I wanted him to talk to me, and I would sit at his feet on the floor, but this time it was my turn to tell him stories I made up. When I saw a flicker in his eyes, I knew he heard me and understood me.

We had less contact with my paternal grandparents. They lived farther away, and although Apu visited them regularly, we children never spent time in their home. Perhaps because after my father's mother, Chava Reichman, died from typhus when my father was ten years old and his sister Ilona was eleven, my grandfather sent him away to a Yeshiva in Balmazujvaros and later to the famous Hunsdorf Yeshiva, and my father never felt again that that place was his home. I heard later that my grandmother lost a seven-year old daughter by drowning, and she became depressed before she died.

My grandfather, Farkas Engel (Zev), was born in 1872, in Hajdudorog, Hungary. He later remarried and had nine more children with his second wife, Hani Roza Haiman. These uncles and aunts would visit us occasionally, but the relationship never developed the closeness we had felt with my mother's family. When I got older, I blamed Anyu for this. I vowed that when I had a family, I would give equal importance to both sets of my children's grandparents; but, tragically, my children never knew three of their grandparents, those who perished in the Holocaust. My father's sister, Ilona, died in Auschwitz, together with her husband, Geza Glucklich. They had two children, Tibor and Eva, but I lost contact with them after the war. I heard that Tibor became a Communist activist in Hungary after the war and Eva emigrated to Australia, married, had a daughter but died a few years later.

Six of my father's half siblings perished in the war. I only know their names but I do not recall their faces: Margit, Rivka, Shmilu, Gizi, Emma, and Hershu. Three of my father's half siblings survived the war. Yitzhak (Geza) had left his wife and his two children in Hungary and went to Palestine when Hitler came to power, with the hope that he would bring his family there later. But the borders closed and his family was trapped in Hungary and perished with the others. One younger brother, Erno, survived in Russia, immigrated to Israel after the war, but died in an accident there, which some people thought was suicide. The youngest sister, Evi, survived in Budapest, got married to Yehuda Grunwald and also went to live in Israel. She is now a widow, has two adult children, several grandchildren and great grandchildren. I try to maintain a relationship with them.

I remember my grandfather, Farkas, as a short man, with a sweet smile who always brought us special "silk" candies when he visited us. He lost his eyesight in his later years, and I always cherished his loving touch on my face when he tried to identify who I was. He was known to be an upright, learned man, but not very successful in business, and his partners often took advantage of him. My father learned honesty and steadfastness in his beliefs from his father. Because their name was Engel, which means angel, my mother often teased my father for not having his feet firmly planted on the ground, and for looking at the world too idealistically.

THE BEGINNING OF THE END

Tearfully, I said goodbye to the Jewish Middle School in Miskolc when I turned fourteen. The excitement of the last days, the final assembly, the honors, the faces of my teachers whom I loved, all melted together into this kaleidoscope of color and sound and whirled around in my head at dizzying speed. My class was the last to graduate, the school now closed for good to comply with the ever-increasing anti-Jewish laws of the city. The classrooms with some 40 desks, the hallways with the pictures of the Hungarian heroes, the large yard where generations of children had chased each other or danced on Hungarian patriotic holidays, now all stood deserted, empty. I took one more look before I ran to catch up with the others.

"Goodbye, goodbye," said my friend Judy, embracing me. "I'll never forget you—you will always be my best friend."

"Please save all your notes for me. I will try to learn everything that they teach you in your new school, 's'il vous plait'—you see, I already started learning French," I said pleadingly.

I tried to act cheerful but as I looked at her pretty face, her golden hair, I knew these were not the things for which I envied her the most any more. It was that she could continue to go to school, something that I ached to do but couldn't.

Her parents got the money together to send her to Debrecen where they had a Jewish gymnasium, or high school. I didn't even dare to mention to my parents that my teachers urged me to continue with my schooling. I was always the best student, never missed a day in school. I excelled in all the subjects, and I earned the recognition I craved. So when it became obvious that my formal schooling had to end, I felt devastated, as if I were shipwrecked, no place to go, no place to express my love of learning or receive the gift of my teachers' instructions and interest in developing my mind.

"These are hard times," Apu said somberly, his forehead creased, as he pushed the newspaper away. "In 1942, here in Hungary, we should be satisfied if we have enough money to pay the bills and have bread on the table."

My father, Jeno Engel (Yakov Koppel in Hebrew) was born in 1897 and had lived through many hard times. After his Yeshiva education he never returned to his hometown, Hajdudorog, but when his family moved to Miskolc, he joined them there and went into his father's textile business. He was a "well-situated" 27-year-old young man, with a good name, when he met my mother through a *Shadchen* (marriage broker) in 1924.

My mother, Malvina Salamonovics (Miriam), was born on December 10th, 1901, a date our family always celebrated by eating Hungarian hot dogs, a specialty at that time. She was 23 when she met my father. She was the second child of my grandparents, one of 13 children, twelve of them alive at the beginning of the war. She was trained in my grandfather's business, acknowledged and respected for her ability and for her loyalty to her father. She was never required to help her mother in the kitchen or with any of the domestic duties. My grandfather always said that it would be a waste of her brain. My mother married my father because her father liked him. He was impressed by his integrity and by his Jewish scholarship. Even though my mother had liked another man, but one who was not as learned in the Talmud as my father, she acceded to my grandfather's wishes and married my father.

After Apu's textile business failed during the depression, he and Anyu struggled to build up the kosher restaurant. Their marriage often echoed past regrets and lost dreams—something we, as children, did not understand; we just felt the undercurrent. My mother was a tireless and capable partner, but showed little affection for my father, which was not unusual because the show of affection was not encouraged in our religious community. I think that emotionally she remained strongly connected to her father, who was her ideal man. Still, my father had always been very solicitous toward my mother. He always behaved as a gentleman, buying her favorite delicacies, opening the door for her, bringing her a sweater when the air became cool. We children saw Apu as a man whose devotion to Anyu was unconditional. He also showed great respect to his father-in-law, perhaps gaining extra favors from my mother.

I had a hard time accepting Apu's explanation as to why I could not continue going to school. My father did not like to deny me anything, but now he felt he needed to tell me how things were. It was difficult for him to disappoint me. I sensed his feeling of frustration and helplessness even if he did not reveal his feelings. He was generally a man of mild manners, thoughtful and compassionate. His guiding principle was the Torah and its commandments.

"Can I at least buy some of their books so that I could study on my own?" I *noodged* my father, who stroked my head and said patiently:

"You don't understand, my daughter, but now we live in a different world. We Jews are no longer the owners of businesses and factories. The peasants and miners who work for your grandfather no longer look up to him with respect. They get their wages, but they never pay for what they buy in his stores." I listened and wondered how everything had turned so bad.

23

"Tell me, Apu, why is Tommy suddenly not allowed to talk to me when I go up to the second floor and knock on his door? They used to invite me to see their Christmas tree every year, and now his mother told me to leave." My father had no answer. He just sighed heavily and walked away.

A few weeks later, in the summer of 1942, Anyu called me into the bedroom and said in a low, nervous voice:

"Tonight there is going to be small wedding in our courtyard. There is a rabbi, who escaped from Poland, who is going to get married to a young woman, who also escaped from Czechoslovakia. This has to be kept a secret, so don't tell anyone."

She had no further explanation why they escaped, why the whole thing was a secret. This was just one more thing I did not understand. I felt annoyed that my parents still treated me as a child, protecting me from something.

The stars shone brightly that evening as the petite, young bride in a white dress and the much older-looking groom dressed in a dark suit, together with ten men, gathered around the four poles of the *huppah* (canopy). I sneaked out of the house and watched them from the far corner of the yard. I heard the blessings recited in hushed tones, then they quickly entered the house for a small meal. There was no singing, no dancing, just the prescribed ceremony, bare, joyless. The couple spent the night in a makeshift bedroom set up in our dining room. At dawn they left silently.

"I wondered why there were no parents or siblings at the wedding," I questioned my mother later, and she answered sadly, "This was the rabbi's second marriage; his first wife and children were killed in Poland. We don't know where their parents are."

A few months later Anyu's younger brother, Erno, was called in for service in the Jewish labor battalions. These battalions were created for Jewish men who did *munkaszolgalat* (slave labor), sometimes attached to certain Hungarian army units, sometimes independent of them. Two of her brothers had already been sent months before to the Russian front with these battalions, and the news from there was generally bad, although we did not hear from them directly. The Jews were not equipped with proper clothing, neither were they fed well, and they were assigned to heavy and dangerous labor; they died quickly from exposure and starvation. But Erno was now in Miskolc, and they were ready to ship him to the East as well. We knew we needed to do something, to prevent this from happening.

We discovered that there was a doctor in Budapest who would supply certain injections that would cause inflammation in the legs that would make it impossible for Erno to walk and thus avoid being shipped out. My parents made arrangements and sent my older brother, Yitzhak, who was a capable 17-year-old young man, to Budapest to pick up the package of injections from the doctor and bring it back to Miskolc. My brother jumped at the opportunity to prove how responsible he was, and although this was a dangerous task, he took it as an exciting challenge.

He left on the train in the morning and, triumphantly, arrived back the same evening with the package. To my surprise, he asked me to go with him to the military hospital where my uncle's unit was stationed. Although he didn't like to admit it, he must have felt safer if someone accompanied him on this risky outing. Finally, I felt useful and needed by my big brother, and I eagerly clutched the precious package in my hand when he handed it to me. Then he and I took the streetcar and traveled to the military hospital.

When we arrived, my brother surveyed the room, instructed me to watch out for anyone observing him. I signaled to him that no attendant was visible, and he got my uncle out of bed; they walked to the bathroom where he stuck the needle with the special substance into my uncle's thigh. The next day my uncle came down with a high fever, and his legs swelled to twice their size. When we visited him that day, his face was contorted from the pain, but he was spared from being shipped out. We gave him the injections a few more times, but when it became too risky, we could no longer continue. Soon he was transferred to another place, but remained inside Hungary. We heard from him that he was having trouble with his leg, but it was a small price to pay for being spared in 1942–1943 from the harsh winter on the Russian front.

Meanwhile in 1942 and 1943, as the months passed, our situation only got worse. Every day new anti-Jewish legislation appeared that further limited our economic and social activities. All Jewish institutions, including schools, were closed. Jewish students were not accepted to the universities. Many businesses that were owned by Jews were either confiscated or had to be transferred to non-Jews. Ritual slaughtering was forbidden, contact with non-Jews curtailed. Christians could no longer be employed by Jews. I spent my days studying, reading, or helping my parents in the restaurant. But we could hardly make a living any more, and soon my father contemplated closing the restaurant altogether. We had to dismiss our cook, Aunt Mari, who had worked for us since 1929 when my parents had first opened the restaurant. Her daughter, "Little" Mari, who had also been living with us since then, swore she would not leave us. She was my older "sister" who was always at my side and who even taught me the delicious "secrets" of adult life, my first class in sex education. But she also had to go.

I was looking for something to keep my mind off the daily attacks on the Jews. When I was told by my friends that young people were gathering in basements at clandestine Zionist meetings, I decided to join them. I never told my parents about it. These meetings were forbidden—if we were discovered, we would be arrested. We sat closely together as we sang Hebrew songs and planned our future in Palestine. We listened to speeches of miraculous escapes by recent refugees from countries that were already occupied by the Germans.

One young man in his early 20s, tall, scholarly looking in his dark-rimmed glasses, told us how he had left his parents in Amsterdam. Someone had come for him in the middle of the night to take him across the border, hoping to escape the fate of other Jews who were being deported to the East. We did not know what he meant by "the East," that there were concentration camps there. He was still hoping that one day he could go back and find his parents or perhaps they would all meet in Palestine. We listened to him in awe, but we really didn't comprehend what was happening to the Jews in those faraway countries. His hope became our prayer. In the outside world, nothing was clear or organized any more, only a state of apprehension and confusion. But here in the darkness of the basement, a ray of sunshine penetrated. We dreamed of redemption.

Sunday, March 19, 1944—It was a mild spring morning, a day that marked the beginning of the end of our lives in Hungary. Anyu had just returned from Edeleny where she had gone to visit her parents every week. Edeleny was only a short 20-kilometer train ride from Miskolc, our home. My grandparents had recently moved back to Edeleny from Budapest where they had lived for a short while, getting better medical care following my grandfather's numerous strokes. But things became difficult in Budapest because of the frequent air raids there. Edeleny had been their lifelong home, where they had raised their twelve children and where my grandfather had employed most of the town in his many businesses.

On that fateful morning my brother Yitzhak woke up early and hurried to catch the train to Budapest to see a soccer game. He was an avid soccer fan and when he got a job, he bought himself a yearly train pass to travel to Budapest on Sunday mornings to watch the game and then return the same day. Budapest was about 180 kilometers from Miskolc. My parents were not happy about these excursions, but my brother was almost 19 now, and they had accepted his passion for the sport. He was a responsible son—he worked at different jobs to help out the family.

On that day my parents were especially anxious because there were rumors that the German army was approaching Hungary. Until then, we made ourselves believe that because the Hungarian government was part of the Axis, a close ally of Germany, it would never be occupied by Germany the way most of the other European countries were already occupied. After all, our government followed all the Nazi laws against the Jews that had affected virtually every aspect of our lives. Most of the adult Jewish males had already been taken into forced labor battalions on the Eastern Front. We trusted that Regent Miklos Horty would protect his patriotic and loyal Jews since we Jews had resided in Hungary for almost a thousand years.

Even when I was younger, we children had often discussed what we overheard from our parents, but we, and our parents as well, had only limited knowledge of what was happening to the Jews in other German-occupied countries. News reached us only through the grapevine, since there was no free press. The government censored the news on the radio, and those who owned radios had to give them up. My father and brothers picked up most of the news in the synagogue, their faces often solemn and anxious when they returned from their daily prayers.

I had a game with my friends, which we called "what if." Each of us had to find a miraculous solution to the problems, and our solutions were not always peaceful. My friend Magda was convinced that the situation would improve only if someone assassinated Hitler. I remember Judy's statements, who heard from her parents that we would be saved only if the Americans and the Soviets won the war and chased the Nazis out of Hungary. I firmly believed that only the coming of the Messiah would save us. We knew that these were just fantasies, but the game gave us some feeling of power. Still, it did not alleviate our fears about the possibility that Germany would occupy Hungary.

It was about noon that day when the news reached us that the German army was marching down Main Street. We stayed in our homes, worried about those who were out on the streets or in public places. We heard that people had to identify themselves to the Nazi officers, and if they had no identification cards, the Germans pulled down the men's pants to see if they were circumcised, since only Jewish males were circumcised in Hungary, and they were arrested.

Evening came and my brother had not returned. Nor did we hear from him during the following days or weeks. No message, no news, nobody knew what had happened to him—he had simply disappeared. There were others who also vanished without a trace on that day. A heavy gloom descended on us, and I could cheer neither my parents nor myself. We walked around the house restlessly, jumping at every knock on the door, suspicious of every person who walked by the window. Weeks later we heard that the Germans had rounded up everyone at the railroad station on that day and had taken them to Kistarcsa, a detention camp near Budapest, where they were incarcerated and tortured. My brother was among those who were arrested at the station, on his way home from the soccer game, and he was taken to Kistarcsa. According to rumors, my uncle Erno, whom we had tried to protect from being shipped out to the Eastern front, also ended up in Kistarcsa.

My younger brother Moshu was 13 then, a skinny, small boy, light skinned and delicate, and, I believed, my mother's favorite. He was my biggest competition for her attention, and he knew how to get it. He would save up money and buy my mother little presents, which she proudly showed to everyone. Although I was jealous of him, I was also very protective of him, because he looked so fragile and was often beaten up by the Gentile boys on his way to Hebrew school. One day he arrived home with blood oozing from his nose and from his ear, his pants torn. I watched him being washed by my mother and stared at the blue veins standing out from his white temples and prayed that no one would hurt him again. I never worried about my older brother because he was tough and muscular and boasted that he was not afraid of anyone.

After my older brother Yitzhak disappeared, my parents decided that they would send Moshu to my grandparents, to Edeleny. Edeleny was a small town, and my mother was convinced that her family could get more food there and that my brother would be better protected from the Gentile boys. One day a woman in a peasant dress appeared at the door and said, "I'll take him now." Apu handed her something, probably money, and without a word, the woman took Moshu's hand and led him away. Moshu did not protest. He did not create a scene the way I, perhaps, would have done. He just looked at us, his face controlled, his body stiff, as he left the house. Anyu stayed in the corner, wiping her eyes for a long time. I wanted to run after him to tell him that I was really not mad at him, that it was okay if he was my mother's favorite. But I was afraid to walk out with the yellow star on my dress, which we all had to wear now. I turned back at the gate of the courtyard as they vanished among the people on the street.

Every day new laws were announced that further limited our lives. One day big signs appeared everywhere, saying:

"From now on all Jews must live within the area that is assigned to be the ghetto. Families who already reside within those boundaries must accommodate those who live elsewhere."

We already lived in the designated area, so the next day two other families moved in with us, and later two more families came to live in our little home. We had a modest apartment—one large bedroom, one dining room that was converted into a second bedroom when we grew bigger, a large kitchen, and a bathroom with a tub and a water heater. There was a separate toilet near the entrance. We usually ate our meals in the spacious entry hall, which was between the kitchen and the restaurant. Our dining room furniture had been moved into the restaurant, which by now had been closed, thus providing a large area where the additional people could be accommodated. The families that moved in with us had many little children as well as aged parents. I did not mind the lack of space and privacy—it was comforting to be together, distracted by the children, by the noise, the bustle.

There were frequent air raids, which forced us to spend a lot of time in the shelter. There we were squeezed in together with more people from the building and with others who ran in from the street when they heard the sirens. The damp walls of the basement, the hard benches near the walls, the suffocating smell of sweat made our stay there very uncomfortable.

One evening Sanyi, my older brother's friend, and whom I secretly admired but who usually paid no attention to me, ran into the yard, breathlessly. Everybody had already gone down to the basement shelter but I was lingering around, breathing in the cool air and the fragrance of the early blooming flowers, enjoying not being with others. It was a beautiful starry night, the light breeze rumpled my hair as I lay on two chairs pushed together in the courtyard, looking up at the twinkling stars. Suddenly I felt a soft touch on my cheeks and two eyes gazing at me; the boy, Sanyi, was standing over me, looking at me, then he bent down and kissed me, ever so gently. I had never been kissed before by a boy. The bombs were falling, the sirens were wailing, while we sat there in the bizarre

31

privacy of the air raid. But soon the air raid was over, and everyone came up from the shelter and were relieved to find me unharmed. The next day Sanyi was taken to a labor camp.

⚜

THE LAVENDER KERCHIEF

The kerchief was a gift from Uncle Isidor. He wasn't really my uncle, but a second cousin of my grandmother. I couldn't comprehend why I received such a beautiful gift; after all, he had many grandchildren, who had all moved into the ghetto to live with us. But they were all little, so what use would any one of them have for a kerchief, I thought, trying to find a reason for my good fortune.

Uncle Isidor owned a big textile store a few blocks away on the main street. The kerchief was probably from his store, which had been taken away and padlocked by the Hungarian authorities. We used to think of Uncle Isidor as the *G'vir*, which in Yiddish meant someone who had a lot of money and power. He also owned the large apartment house where my best friend, Judy, lived with her parents and four siblings, and where I often visited on Saturday afternoons. When Uncle Isidor's family moved in with us, they brought with them whatever they could; they even brought butter, which they would spread on bread for the little children. I must have looked hungrily at the yellowish-white butter with the little water bubbles that were still left after the churning of the cream. I stared at the children as they stuffed the bread into their mouths, and Aunt Seren, the stately wife of Uncle Isidor, asked me: "Would you like some butter on your bread?"

"No," I replied. I was too embarrassed to admit how much I wanted it. I had not seen butter since the last time a farmer had paid my grandfather with butter for the lumber he bought from him, years before.

Uncle Isidor's gift was like something that did not belong in the ghetto, where everything was stuffy, gray, and dirty; it looked as if it weren't made of fabric at all, but of real live flowers. I could almost smell their fragrance, waiting for a butterfly to land on it. The purple petals of the hydrangeas intertwined with the pinks of the roses and the blues of the petunias, jutting out of the snow-white background. I decided that, for simplicity's sake, I would call it the Lavender Kerchief. I did not care that there was no lavender color in it. To me it looked lavender. I walked around in the ghetto, proudly showing off my treasure.

I never had a pale lavender anything, never a dress that had even resembled anything pastel, something I had always longed for. The dark navy school uniform—and even my summer dress of ugly green and maroon stripes that was a remake from my aunt's old dress—made me feel grave and ancient. I wanted to be young and carefree. I didn't mind the navy uniform so much; after all, it was something that tied me to the group, to the school that I happily used to go to every day. After the school was closed, I had the uniform remodeled into a regular navy dress and wore it every Shabbat. But the striped rayon dress made me feel as if I must carry the burden of a somber, older generation. Now I finally got something light, a fresh breath of spring, something pretty, even frivolous.

One day there was an announcement that a few girls were needed to go to work for a Bulgarian farmer outside the ghetto, away from the city. I jumped at the opportunity and volunteered. I was eager to escape from the stiflingly crowded rooms, the unkempt streets, and the anxious chatter of the adults. I fantasized as if we would be going on an outing, or even to a celebration. I was

15, and I wanted to wear my lavender kerchief, to dress up, to look pretty. But Anyu was displeased.

"It is dangerous to wear this outside the ghetto. What if a German soldier notices you; he might take you with him to their headquarters. And even if that doesn't happen, he may take the kerchief away from you to send back home to his girlfriend. Besides, the Bulgarian farmer could accuse you of having stolen the kerchief and denounce you. Why take chances?" My mother could think of endless problems that wearing the kerchief would cause.

"I don't care! It won't happen," I answered, and no amount of warnings made me change my mind. The very next morning, as the truck came to pick us up to take us to the farm, I tied the kerchief tightly around my face and felt protected from the chill of dawn. The April wind sent shivers through my bones in the open truck, as we, 15 teenage girls, huddled together on the floor of the truck. I held on to the lavender kerchief even tighter.

At the farm I dug and planted potatoes, row after row, all day long. The earth felt strange to my fingers, often muddy, reminding me of the dough my grandmother taught me to knead for bread. But now there was no more flour to knead, and I did not know how my grandmother was, or if she would ever teach me anything again. I wanted so much to touch her veined hands, to receive her praise for something well done.

"Here is your bread," said the Bulgarian farmer roughly, as he interrupted my musing about my grandmother at the end of the long day. His large body loomed above me, covering up the last rays of the setting sun. I quickly got up and hurried to the waiting truck. I got a whole loaf as payment for my work, and I wanted to take it back to the ghetto. I held the bread under my arm carefully, as if it were a baby, as I climbed up onto the truck. I felt strong and accomplished, so proud that I could bring something home to my family. The ride home was long, the fragrance of the bread crust teased my nostrils, and my belly became more and more demanding. I arrived back to the ghetto and hung my head as I handed Anyu just half of the loaf of bread.

A few weeks passed and then Apu was called in to be taken to the forced labor camp. My father was among the last ones; most of the other men were already gone. Anyu baked some Hungarian cookies called *pogacsa* with our last bits of flour. The morning he was to leave, he struggled to pack it in his backpack, together with some warm clothes, because he did not know if he would be back before the cold winter. When he tried to put on his backpack he staggered under its weight; his body had been trained to sit at the table and pore over his books of Talmud. The heaviest thing he had ever lifted was a tray of food, while serving the guests in our restaurant, or a basket of vegetables when he returned from the market. I suddenly thought of the restaurant that had been closed a while ago, and remembered the traveling salesmen who used to eat there but who now stopped selling, stopped traveling, and many had stopped eating—everything had changed.

On that morning Apu stood bent at the door, the pale skin of his arms matched the whiteness of his face. The blue-colored work shirt that he borrowed from the janitor, because he only owned white shirts, looked strange on him. I waited for him to say something, words of promise, of hope, but his embrace was silent. I, too, held my lips tightly closed. I was afraid that if I opened my mouth, I would cry like an abandoned child. Anyu kept herself busy; she did not allow herself to show any weakness. I knew way down at the core of my being as I watched him trudge away that my gentle, saintly father would not survive. I feared that his trust in human beings would lead him to disappointment and even to betrayal. I imagined that he would share his bread with another who, he thought, was even hungrier than he, and he would die of hunger.

A few weeks later it was announced that all the Jews of the ghetto would be relocated to the "Brickyard," outside the city. The time had finally come for my mother and me to say goodbye to our home. We were ordered one day to pack up whatever we were able to carry on our backs and to line up in our courtyard, together with all the others who lived and stayed with us in the building. Anyu decided a few days before to hide her jewelry in the cellar, under the coal. We also carried down the heavy volumes of my father's Talmud and buried them there. "What if they find all this?" I questioned her, and she answered confidently: "The war will be over before they use up all this coal; my father had always provided us with enough coal to warm our home with and now there won't be anyone else to use it." My mother always knew everything absolutely, and if she believed it, I did too. Even my father had rarely argued with her, because he trusted her more than he trusted himself.

The following morning we lined up in our courtyard. We knew that it signaled the time when we would be transferred to the brickyard, an area where they dried the bricks that were manufactured there. "How can my grandchildren walk that far?" lamented Aunt Seren, worriedly. "We don't have enough arms to carry all of them." Anyu took charge, immediately, and arranged people to help.

Soon the Hungarian gendarmes entered the yard. "Do you have any money or jewelry hidden anywhere?" I heard the rough words as I fixed my stare at his rooster-feathered hat. I felt his hands going over my body, then he motioned to his woman assistant who dug her fingers into the secret parts of my body, searching for hidden gold. When no treasures were found, just to make sure we understood the seriousness of trying to hide something, he swished his whip over my head and left fat welts on my back. I glanced toward my mother and was amazed at the frank expression of anger on her face, but not fear.

I had my backpack at my feet, all ready, in it everything that was important to me—my picture album, my diary, the notes that I had copied from the books I loved. We were already at the gate of the courtyard when Anyu realized that I had not packed my sweater or any food. "Your head is always on foolish things," she reprimanded me with increasing apprehension. Suddenly, she didn't look so confident to me, but she did not utter a word of despair. She was wearing her holiday dress, her head covered by a silk scarf, and her walk was erect, determined. She didn't know that I had hidden my beloved lavender kerchief way on the bottom of the pack where, I was sure, no one could find it and no one could ever take it from me.

With one last look at the geranium boxes in the kitchen window, we closed the heavy gate to our courtyard and started to walk with the others in the middle of the street. I looked ahead of us and then behind. There was a multitude of people, carrying their bundles, their little children, helping the old to walk. The gendarmes surrounded the columns of people on both sides of the street; their bayonets glinted in the sunshine.

No one waved goodbye to us.

᪗

THE BRICK FACTORY — "Crossing the Threshold"

The train always stopped at the top of the hill. It brought the Jews from the surrounding towns and villages to join us in the brickyard. We camped down below, much like I had seen gypsies spread out at the end of the village where my grandparents had lived. We had come by foot, our bundles on our backs that held all our worldly possessions. The lavender kerchief remained securely hidden in the bottom of my backpack. There were women, some nursing babies, and children everywhere. They divided the modest food they brought along among their offspring. I roamed around between the covered shelters where bricks used to be stacked for drying. I needed to use the bathroom but could not find it. When I asked some older people, they pointed to the hill where there were a few bushes and trees. "Make sure you stay over on that side," one said. "That's for girls."

I looked at her in disbelief. "People can see me there," I exclaimed, but I sensed that there would be no further explanation and went to look for the place. The image of my father appeared in front of me, his expression serious, fatherly. "Remember, my daughter, modesty is very important. Dress always in such a way that you don't attract unwanted looks, that you stay humble and not boastful.

And if any of the soldiers are around, it's best if you hide somewhere, or try to look like an old woman."

What should I do now? All around me were swarms of people, older men, and mostly young Hungarian guards everywhere. "Apu, you never told me about this," I said out loud, but my father was no longer there, his image had faded away, and I was facing the trunk of a big tree. I stepped forward, stretched my arms out, and embraced the tree, its brown bark scraping my soft inner arm, and I held on to its solid hardness.

The following day a few of us got together and dug some trenches in a fairly well protected area, which from then on was recognized as the "Ladies' Room." I learned to use it like everyone else.

Then we organized a community kitchen. Everyone brought something and we made a fire in a kettle, and somebody found a grate to put on top of it. Soon the delicious aroma of fried onions filled the air. We surrounded the kettle with our bread in our hands and waited patiently until our turn came to spread the onions on top of the bread. "Never have I eaten such wonderful food before," I reassured Anyu, who handled the situation with characteristic efficiency, but I saw that her face had acquired more shadows.

The soldiers were quite friendly, and one of them volunteered some information for us after my mother gave him a ring that she had somehow hidden in the seam of her dress.

"Soon you'll be transported to a working camp, where you will be treated well. The old people and the children will be taken care of while you work, and you will be together in the evening."

"But where will they take us?" my mother asked anxiously.

"To somewhere, maybe to Germany, maybe to Poland, I don't know, but away from here." He looked uncomfortable about his geography but I felt more optimistic.

"There must be a better place, not so disorganized, someone who will give us directions, tell us what to do," I turned to Anyu, expecting her reassurance, but none came.

Then people started receiving postcards. "We arrived well, and we are fine, we have work and they treat us well." Family members from other cities who lived in the northern part of Hungary signed the cards. We looked at the cards doubting that they were genuine, until one woman exclaimed: "This card is from my brother who used to live near the Tatra Mountains. If he sent this card, then it must be true." The straw on the cement floor did not feel so scratchy that night.

The third day more transports started to arrive on top of the hill. They had emptied the ghettos of the surrounding area and brought the people here. We watched as the big doors of the cattle cars opened and out poured old and young, their faces bewildered, confused. A fence separated me from the train, but when I saw my grandparents being pushed out of the car, I impulsively climbed over the fence, gathered all my strength, lifted my grandfather and carried him on my back down the hill. My grandmother, led by my aunt, walked down slowly with her cane. Her face was blank, white. My grandfather was semi-conscious, having suffered several strokes in the recent past. I secured a blanket and spread it on the thin layer of straw that served as a bed in the open-sided brick-shed. My grandfather, the revered patriarch of the family, the man who had been respected by all, and who had given employment to the whole village, now lay there on the straw like a beaten animal. His starched white shirt collar was wrinkled around his neck, his black suit covered with dirt. His once sparkling black eyes now stared vacantly into the air. He mumbled garbled words.

The world that I had known kept falling apart. I stroked my grandfather's face, and I repeated the story that he had often told me: "This is the beginning of our promised redemption; before the arrival of the Messiah, we will be rolling down the mountain, and soon we'll arrive at the place where the bread grows on trees." This is how I heard it from him as a little child. I wanted to comfort him, but I also wanted to believe, desperately, that it would really happen and that the redemption would soon be here.

Five of my aunts and their little children also came with the transport. Four of them were married, but their husbands had been taken away to forced labor camps a long time ago. My aunt Reggie's husband, Feri, was among them. Reggie had four children, but only two, Marta and Shanyi, were with her; the oldest son, Ancsi, fourteen, was also taken into the forced labor battalion, together with my younger brother, Moshu, whom we had sent to Edeleny in the hope that he would be safer there. My aunt's second child, Suri, was just twelve when the Jews of Edeleny were herded into the local ghetto.

"Suri made up her mind that she would not go into the ghetto, and I could not convince her otherwise," said my Aunt Reggie, her voice choked. "The next day Suri was dead. The doctor said it was something like a cerebral hemorrhage, very unusual for a child her age. But I know that she willed her death because she did not want to go to the ghetto." We listened to my aunt in a state of shock.

My Aunt Margit was also there, together with her four little boys—Imre, Ervin, Bandy, and a baby. My uncle Jeno was taken away two years before. Aunt Margit was a beautiful woman and because she had only boys, she often attempted to make me pretty; she would comb my hair and give me colorful ribbons. Once a year, on the Purim holiday, she would send me a doll.

My Aunt Manci held her little boy, Zoltan, who had just learned to walk. Her husband, my Uncle Miksha, had also been taken to the eastern front a long time before. My uncle Hermus was also taken into the forced labor battalions. His pregnant wife, Editke, was also with us in the brickyard.

My youngest aunt, Lilli, was not yet married, so the care of my grandparents was largely her responsibility. She was relieved to find us in the brickyard and told us how the people in Edeleny had turned against them; no one offered to help them, nobody came to give them any assistance. They even joined the known anti-Semites in ridiculing and humiliating them. She told us how two peasants grabbed my grandfather and cut his beard while the others laughed.

Having more of my extended family with us was comforting, but also gave us more to worry about. I was especially concerned about my grandfather and wanted to do everything to make him more comfortable. I spent hours crouching next to him on the floor, singing softly the old melodies that he had loved so much. Sometimes he reacted with a smile, but other times he seemed so far away it was as if his eyes already saw the world to come.

I soon realized that the shed in which my grandparents had been placed was designated as the "hospital." Besides my grandparents, there were between 30 and 40 sick, old people lying on the floor, no one paying attention to them. They had emptied the hospitals of all the Jews and now they were brought here, without families. A group of us got together, and it became clear that now we, young girls, had a task to perform: we transformed ourselves into nurses without uniforms, without any knowledge of injuries or illnesses or how to take care of sick, elderly people. But we knew that this was our job now. We became their caretakers, and suddenly I saw that I could be useful, that there was some purpose to my life.

It took some effort to overcome my revulsion at first. There was one large man, his face drawn, his eyes bulging, his mouth gaping. I clutched my stomach, wanting to throw up, but was able to control myself and got closer to him with a bowl of soup. I put his coat under his head to raise him so I could feed him with the spoon and he could swallow the lukewarm liquid. "Whose grandpa are you?" I asked him, but he could only look at me, voiceless. The liquid ran out of the side of his mouth, and I tried to catch it with the spoon—a mother feeding a baby—I thought, and instinctively, I smiled at him.

"What do we do about their diapers?" my friend questioned me. I looked around for someone to tell me what to do, but there were only my friends and I. I understood that the whole responsibility was upon us and that we had taken that on, voluntarily. I think that that was the moment when I crossed the threshold from the innocence of childhood into the dark unknown of the adult world.

When the order came to board the train on the hill, I left my "patients," and they were carried up to the train by others. I was with my mother and some cousins, but my grandparents were put into the adjacent car with the other sick people. Now my Aunt Lilli assumed the role of the nurse so she could stay with my grandparents. I still held on to my backpack, my lavender kerchief safely tucked in; the backpack was now lighter because we did not have any more food with us.

The cattle car was filled with humans, squashed together, without space to sit. A few feet away I was surprised to see our neighbor whom we knew to be a Christian. He hated us children if we stepped on the grass in front of his house, and he used to chase us away, calling us dirty Jewish kids. Now he was leaning against a young woman, perhaps his daughter, his face ashen, empty of any emotion. I wished I could have shaken him, reminding him that he could not escape, that Hitler considered him a Jew even though he and his father had converted to Christianity. Or just tell him anything, to wake him. I wanted to hear him cursing us again, but words did not come from his lips.

The massive door of the car was bolted, the whistle blew, and the train pulled away. No one told us where we were going. Someone pointed to the pail a few feet away, saying it was there to be used as a toilet. I thought back to the trenches we had dug in the brickyard and wondered if it could get even worse.

It was the third day on the train when it suddenly stopped. I felt that the air had somehow leaked out of the cattle car and there was nothing left to breathe. My mother tried to get me to the narrow slit of the barred window but I couldn't get through. Then I noticed an opening to my right; I looked down and saw the head of my friend Judy's little sister, Toby. Toby was way down there, by our feet; I tried to grab her golden curls to lift her up, but the train started to move again and I let go of her hair. I watched her but she did not move, I called her but she did not answer. I almost reached her at the next jerk of the train, but again she slipped out of my hands. I felt desperate. Why wasn't someone helping her? How could I explain to my friend that I let go of Toby's hair?

Finally, Mrs. Gross, who was right next to me, whispered in my ear, glancing over the golden curls: "She is gone, there is no air down there, there is just no air, there is nothing you can do." I looked at her as if I did not understand what she said. Did Toby just stop being because there was no air? Why couldn't someone get her to the window? Why couldn't her mother hold her, the way some other babies were held? Where was her mother? I looked around and realized that there were fewer little children than on the first day after we left the brickyard. I saw women with empty arms and empty faces. After three days of not eating or sleeping their arms must have gotten tired and they let go of their precious possessions. Or perhaps the children were crushed by all that pushing and shoving.

I could not stop agonizing over it. I heard the wheels of the train clanking, and then I must have dozed off. The shrill sound of the whistle aroused me from my stupor and suddenly the train came to a screeching halt.

"SEE YOU LATER, GRANDMA" —
Auschwitz–Birkenau

AUSCHWITZ-BIRKENAU the sign read at the station. The name did not look familiar from my geography book. Finally the heavy bolts of the doors were removed and the front of the car opened. "*Los, los, alle heraus,*" I heard the harsh, loud command of the uniformed SS as we scrambled down the plank, being pushed from the inside and yanked by our arms by strange-looking men in striped clothes and caps. "Leave your belongings in the train and line up on the road next to the tracks," they instructed us. I was trying to hold on to my backpack with my lavender kerchief in it, but a guard quickly pushed me down. When I hit the floor I looked around and saw thousands of people standing next to the railroad cars, women holding on to their children, pushed and shoved by vicious-looking *Kapos,* prisoners themselves who were selected especially because of their criminal backgrounds, to keep the new arrivals under control. In the distance I saw funny-looking people who were gesticulating to us as if they wanted to deliver a message. "I think they are inmates in an insane asylum," I said to my mother, who was somewhere behind me. The music of Strauss was faintly audible, and far away there were houses with flower gardens.

My mother was holding her cousin's baby in her arms. Then I saw her talking to a man in prison garb and handing the baby over to the mother. There was tremendous confusion. Mothers were looking for their children, trying not to be separated from them. Then I saw my mother near the "hospital" car, standing next to my grandmother. I thought she wanted to make sure that they would be taken care of. My grandfather was not visible; he was probably lying on the floor, unable to get up, perhaps unconscious. The Nazi officers in spotless uniforms and shiny boots, surrounded with vicious-looking dogs, snapped their whips over our backs, urging us to hurry up, calling us dirty swine and cursed Jews. The German language that I had learned in school, the beautiful poems of Goethe and Schiller, did not sound like this. I felt frightened by their harshness, the words echoed the snapping of their whips. I was sure that the world, the whole world, had gone mad, and I wondered if we had all descended into hell.

But I had no time to give in to my ruminations. I quickly fell in line with the others and moved hurriedly ahead. Still, as if pulled by a magnet, I looked back and waved to my grandmother, the mother of twelve children, and the grandmother of 15, who never uttered an unkind word in her life. She was just standing there, leaning on her cane, a small figure in her dark summer dress, a whisper of a smile on her face masking her utter bewilderment. "I'll see you later, Grandma," I yelled. For my transgression for looking back the sharp pain of the whip hit my face again. Even then I was sure that I would see her and my grandfather, later, as we had been told back in the brickyard.

I passed in front of the Nazi officer, Dr. Mengele (I found out his name later), who looked me over and then motioned with his thumb to go to the right. I saw that some others were sent to the left. The image of the handsome figure of Dr. Mengele, in his well-pressed uniform and polished black boots, whose face did not show cruelty, just void of any expression while directing the women left or right, remained with me throughout the years to come. It penetrated my consciousness as a feared symbol of deception and lies, just like the classical music that greeted us upon our arrival at Auschwitz became the dissonant resonance of cruelty and murder.

We were already a few hundred yards ahead of the Nazi officer when I saw Anyu running after the line. She stopped in front of Dr. Mengele, spoke to him briefly. Then she too joined the line to the right where she caught up with me.

"What happened? Why did you leave Grandma?" I asked.

Normally, my mother would always be there to help my grandparents, even leaving her family at home to assist them if needed. That's the way we were all trained.

"She'll be all right. We will see her and Grandpa in the evening when we return from work; that's what we were told. Grandma insisted that I not leave you alone, unsupervised, with so many soldiers around. So I convinced that German officer that I was strong and was capable of working, and he sent me here. I felt bad that I had to give the baby back to his mother; she had another young child she was holding, and she begged me to stay with her, but the man in the striped uniform told me I must return the baby so I could go to work."

She did not realize that her wise mother's advice, and her *chutzpa* to run after me and address Dr. Mengele, saved her life at that moment. I sighed with great relief to have my mother with me again.

I kept my eyes forward on the line in front of me and tried to avoid further blows. I saw long columns of women. The men must have been separated and taken on another road. We did not know what happened to those who were sent to the left. There were no children in our column; I was probably the youngest. Neither were there older women, or mothers with children. They all stayed behind or were sent to the left. Anyu said that her sister, Reggie, could have come with us if she would have left her children with my other aunt, but she wouldn't. At least Aunt Lilli was with us.

I looked back one more time, but the figures of my grandma, my aunts, and my little cousins slowly faded away. I never looked up to see the chimney that was bellowing its red flame and foul-smelling black smoke. I just followed the line.

We marched on the road until we reached a building made of stone blocks. We were quickly ushered into a large room and told to get undressed. It took a while for me to understand the instructions even though I understood German. It seemed unbelievable that they would ask us to shed all our clothes in front of a swarm of Nazi soldiers and Kapos. I took my clothes off, folded them neatly the way I was taught by my mother, but left my underwear on. The next minute I was hit on my back, and the Nazi guard yelled: "You take off everything, do you understand?" I looked around and saw that Anyu was stepping out of her underwear, and for the first time in my life, I saw her body completely naked.

Then I saw all the women and girls, fat and skinny, young and not so young, shedding their clothes, until I no longer saw them as women, only an assemblage of white bodies. Some of them left their sanitary belts on. I felt the world was spinning; shame rolled down my body, from my forehead to my big toes. I had never seen nude people, either in real life or in books or movies. Have we all gone mad? We were all taught, even commanded, not to expose our bodies in public. Again, my father's face appeared before my eyes for a minute, but I did not want to see him. I covered my face. Then my mother's whisper brought me back to our new reality and I understood. I threw my panties on top of the heap and held my hands, defensively, on the lower part of my body.

Exhausted, and shivering, I sat down on the cement floor, leaned against my mother, and soon my head slipped down, and I lay there. I fixed my gaze on the single, naked light bulb hanging from the high ceiling and fell asleep. I awoke to the sounds of loud crying, screaming coming from everywhere, in total darkness. "Where is my Mama?" came the distressed sobbing from behind me. "My God, they took my children," cried another. "Who will look after them?" The long piercing wails filled the room as others echoed the same panic: "Where is my precious Yankele, who will feed my baby Malkele?" and another lamented, "I shouldn't have left my parents all alone. God will punish me for this." Then I heard my friend Judy crying, "Mommy, don't leave me! I'll be good!" Suddenly the light went on and the harsh voice of the German woman soldier jarred us back to our senses. "Quiet, or you'll all be punished." I snuggled up to my mother and covered my ears. I didn't dare move. The light went off.

The next day they made us march out, leaving all our clothes there on the floor. We were taken into the shower house where they shaved the hair on our heads and on our bodies, sprayed us with disinfectant, and ordered us to shower. At this time we had no knowledge of a certain "shower house" that was actually the gas chamber, so we welcomed the water. After the shower we had to stand outside for hours, wet, naked. Finally we were given clothes to wear, not our own, of course, but dresses salvaged from the earlier arrivals. The dresses did not fit; we received no underwear or shoes. I got a large woman's dress, brown and green, certainly not lavender. Anyu got a long, black evening gown, quite transparent, with a many-colored flower design. I stared at her as she stood there in her gown, her hair shaven. I did not want to recognize her; I felt that I had entered another world that existed way down below our world.

Then I looked at the others, the grotesquely dressed, pathetic group, their bare heads blinding my eyes, and I broke out in laughter. I tried to control myself, but I couldn't. I erupted with the force of a volcano, and the laughter spread until everyone exploded in a great hysterical outburst. We looked at each other incredulously, and we touched each other to make sure we were real. Then, as the wave of hysteria diminished, I started to cry. The tears came rolling down my cheeks, they clouded my vision, and choked my voice; I wiped my eyes with the back of my hand. Then I bent down and tore off the bottom of Anyu's gown and I covered her head with the material; I just had to do something that gave me a sense that I could change the feeling of my utter helplessness and chaos into some action for order.

From the shower we proceeded down the road toward the barracks. Row after row of barracks lined the road, high barbed wire fences separated this camp from the next; every few hundred feet there were guard towers. Since we had no shoes, it was painful to walk on the gravel road but eventually, we arrived at our barrack. This was a big stone barn-like building, no furniture, no beds, nothing. We collapsed onto the cement floor, I on top of my mother, Lilli next to me, my best friend Judy next to her, curled up and turned toward the wall.

At dawn we were awakened by the *Blockalteste*, the woman who was in charge of the barrack. She was also an inmate who had been there for a long time. After receiving some dark liquid, which was called coffee, they ordered us to go outside for the roll call, or *Zahl-Appel*. We lined up in front of the building in rows of fives, hundreds of rows of ludicrously-dressed women, thousands of newly shaven white heads glistening in the early morning sun, and I burst out laughing again. I was quickly stopped by the whip of the guard and looked at the others who understood the rules better than I: No talking, no moving, and certainly no laughing was permitted while we waited standing in the *Zahl-Appel*, to be counted by the commandant several hours later. The sun was already high in the sky when the commandant arrived on horseback. We were counted and dismissed. The *Zehl-Appel* was repeated morning and evening, every day.

At midday our food finally arrived. We were famished because for days we had nothing to eat. Every row of five got a pot, in it a grayish mass called soup, to be shared by the five of us. Since we had no bowls or spoons we sat on the floor and passed the pot around. Anyu handed me the pot, which I first allowed to pass by me, but the second time around I closed my eyes and took a mouthful. I quickly covered my mouth to keep the food in and not spit it out. Then I handed the pot to Judy, but Judy would not open her mouth. She held her lips tightly shut when the pot came around the third time—Judy would not take a gulp.

"Please, Judy, please, open your mouth and swallow," I begged her.

"No, I don't want any!" and she pushed the pot away.

"But you must if you want to live," I reasoned with her.

I was desperate. Judy was my best friend since nursery school, the oldest child of five children, the one with whom I always competed, the one I envied because she was more beautiful, had nicer clothes, and had a more permissive mother. Only in sports was I better than she—I could always outrun her.

"Please, Judy, try!" I was on the verge of crying.

"I don't want to live. If I can't be with my family, I don't want to live."

Her terse words pierced my heart. I felt guilty because I had my mother with me. Judy never touched the food, then or after. My beautiful and talented friend had given up competing for life. One day she was taken out of our barrack, and we never saw her again. I wished I could have been with her in her last hours. She died of starvation of the body and of the soul. For many years after the war, I kept dreaming that I was running with her and then leaving her behind.

On about the tenth day after our arrival at Auschwitz, perhaps in the beginning of July, 1944, we were suddenly given the order to march to the showers. After the cold water dried on our backs, we all stood in line and got gray prison garb with numbers on the left side of the dress and wooden-soled canvas shoes. We also received a slice of bread with a piece of sausage on it and were put on the train. We had no idea where we were going or what plans the Nazis had for us, but we were glad that we were leaving Auschwitz, and we hoped that they would transport us to a working camp where we would have a chance to survive.

"DON'T EVER LET THEM SEE YOU CRY" —
Plasow

Again we boarded the cattle cars, and I held on to Anyu and Lilli, and felt very fortunate that we were not separated. The ride took only a few hours. We huddled together on the floor of the car, ate our bread and tried to calm each other. I no longer had any other possessions, no backpack, no diary, and no lavender kerchief. There were some other young women from Miskolc, my hometown, and from Edeleny, where my aunt had lived. It was comforting to be together, but no one talked about our families, whom we had left in Auschwitz, as if we had an agreement that the awful truth could not be spoken. Instead, we talked about our families as if we had just left them home and as if we were going on a vacation to some exotic place. We even recalled cities and therapeutic baths that our parents or grandparents had visited in "good times" and wondered if our voyage would take us in that direction. When the train stopped and we scrambled out of the cars, we read the sign on the station, PLASOW, which we later learned was a suburb of Krakow, Poland, some hundred kilometers east of Auschwitz.

The sun was setting over the hills, and we saw the outlines of the camp, rows of barracks, some on hills, some on level ground. There were no fences between the barracks, and the place looked smaller than Auschwitz, and more open. Men and women were working together. They were Polish Jews, someone said later, who were concentrated there in the ghetto. Our first impression was significantly influenced by our envy of the women prisoners' unshaven heads.

"Look, they have hair! This must be a better place," I said enthusiastically.

"You are always the optimist," said my mother, and a faint smile brightened her face.

Our wooden barrack had rows of three-tiered bunks, a few of us on each level. There was a long table in the middle of the room with benches on both sides where we could sit and eat. Again, I saw that as a good sign. "We are going to eat like human beings!" I declared. I learned that we could get some pots from a large heap of discarded dishes at one end of the camp, and I hurried to find some usable ones for us. I was rummaging through when I felt someone near me. I turned around and saw a young, tall boy, about my age, who was also looking for pots.

[Steven Spielberg has memorialized this place in his movie "Schindler's List," in which a German industrialist set up a factory manufacturing pots and was able to save two thousand Jews from being murdered.]

"These are discards from a factory, and some came from the ghetto," the boy informed me. He paused for a minute and then said: "A week ago I still had my parents and my little brother and sister with me, but the Germans needed space for the new working transports, and they got rid of all the 'useless' people. I watched as they machine-gunned my family, and I could not help them." His face was drawn but controlled.

The Nazis needed to make room for us, I thought, and these families had to be killed in order to bring our transport there. I couldn't believe that some little child had to die so that I could have his wooden plank. Would it be my fault? I wondered, and I felt an icy grip in my chest on that hot summer day. Nothing seemed to make sense any more. Before I could utter a word, I felt the sharp pain of the whip on my back, and the *Kapo* shouted:

"No talking, you swine." I doubled over and started to cry. I don't know if the tears were a reaction to the pain of the whip, to the anguish of the boy's sorrow, or, perhaps, to the unbearable torment of my guilt. The boy managed to whisper in my ear:

"Don't ever let them see you cry," and walked away.

At that moment I stopped envying the girls with their long hair whose families were killed before their very eyes.

Summer in Plasow dragged on with hot days and freezing nights. Early morning wake-up, standing in line for some hot liquid, then in line to be counted on the *Zahl-Appel*, then to be assigned to different work units, often changing daily. There were days when we carried huge rocks recently hewn by the male prisoners, piling them up high in one place. Then, making a human chain, we passed them from hand to hand and loaded them into wagons. My mother tried to protect me by swinging the heavy rock to the person next to me, skipping over me. "She is so young and she is just skin and bone," my mother explained, but I felt embarrassed by her protection. When the next job was to carry an armful of army uniforms on a narrow plank over a deep ravine, my mother's face was terror stricken as she watched me crossing to the other side on steady legs while others, less able, lost their balance and fell into the ravine. The guards kept laughing and snapping their whips, yelling "*schneller, schneller*," faster, faster. I wondered what made me get there safely. Was it my mother's prayer, my wish to have my mother see me strong, or my will to show them, the Nazis, that I could do it?

We were issued new shoes because the old ones were torn from the rocks. "We can't wear these," yelled Lilli as we discovered with horror that the shoes were made of Torah parchments. We called a meeting that evening in the dark, and Anyu, the oldest of the group, decreed: "We must wear the shoes; otherwise we cannot go to work, and it will cost our lives. But let us recite the *Kaddish*, because the destruction of the Torah is like the death of a loved one."

Summer was at its height, and large black flies were buzzing around the discarded horse bones in the garbage. We searched for those that still had some meat on them and returned triumphantly to our barracks with the bones and other edible refuse. Many girls became ill, and some died. It was then that Anyu started to develop a fever every afternoon and would shake all night, burning up. Perhaps it was from the refuse we ate, but I thought it must be malaria, because I learned in school that malaria brings fever every afternoon. Another big problem was the bedbugs that invaded us as soon as the lights were turned off. I often scooped them out of my sunken cheeks where they liked to nest. Their bites caused sores on our bodies, which then became infected. Anyu's legs were especially inflamed, and I stole tissue paper from the infirmary to cover her sores and protect them from the flies, since she had little strength to help herself.

We wanted to keep ourselves clean, but there was never enough water to wash ourselves, and even less to launder our clothes. Still, when I could, I would sneak into the washroom at dawn, take off my dress, wash it then put it back on, still wet. It dried on the way to work; it gave my body a cool relief from the scorching sun. We made a song about this to the tune of a famous Nazi *schlager* (song), and while we pushed the heavy wagons filled with stone, we hummed the tune, without the words, sure that we had outwitted our enemies.

Every day we heard explosions and gunfire in the distance. The Polish Jews were able to receive underground news, which kept us hoping that the war was near the end and that we would be liberated. One day the sounds of mortar guns sent us into ecstasy, and we waited for the Soviets to break through. But evening came, the sirens wailed, and we were ordered a *Zahl-Appel.* We all lined up in the public square, as three prisoners who had tried to escape to meet the advancing Soviet army were caught, and were led to the gallows. One of the three was the boy I met on the first day when I was looking for a pot. I remembered what he said: "Don't ever let them see you cry." I covered my eyes in order not to see the hangings, but I could not stop the aching of my heart, and I cried and cried.

One night there was another general alarm. The large square in the middle of the camp was full of prisoners.

"What now?" we asked each other.

"There is going to be a line-up and they will shoot every tenth person," said Rose, the all-knowing daughter of the rabbi from the Western part of Hungary.

"I know it. I heard it from the men when they carried in our food tonight. They know it. They get reliable information through their spies. I am not going to wait for them to shoot me. I am going back to my barrack. Let them come and get me."

She walked back but before she reached the door a shot was fired. She fell to the ground without a sound.

The announcement came through the loudspeaker. "All units line up and march to the railroad station. Nobody can stay behind." To emphasize the announcement, the sirens wailed and gunshots were fired. We arrived at the station in the darkness of the starless night. Our rations were handed out as we

59

climbed up the planks into the cattle cars. The last girl in our unit, Magda, saw that there was one ration left over in the *Kapo*'s hand. She thought of asking for it, then remembered Rose, the portion that was never to be eaten by her, and she changed her mind and quickly climbed up the plank. We sat on the floor of the car in the darkness, eating our food silently, feeling the emptiness that Rose had left behind. The train started to move.

ॐ

ONCE MORE DR. MENGELE — Auschwitz

The train moved slowly toward the West. The sound of the mortar fire receded and with it our hope that we would be freed by the Russians.

"Maybe we'll be taken to another working camp," said Vali, one of the five in our row for the line-up. She was a distant relative, younger than my mother, but an adult with a practical mind. The train stopped and the heavy doors of the cars opened. The sign AUSCHWITZ-BIRKENAU was devastating to see.

"Oh, no, it cannot be! We were supposed to go to a working camp, not back to the place where Mengele decides who will live and who will die." Vali's voice cracked—she did not appear to be the source of hope she had been just hours before.

While we were in Plasow, we learned about the fate of all those who were sent to the left, and we knew that our physical condition was now much worse after months of slave labor. Gone were our illusions and false hopes about this place of death. The chimney smoke that hit our nostrils as we were pushed out of the train meant that the killing was going on full force and that we could be the next victims. Still I fantasized that maybe we will see my grandparents, that somehow they were left alive.

As we jumped to the ground, we saw barrels of water and ran to them to quench our thirst and soothe our parched lips. When an SS soldier saw this, he kicked the barrel over, spilling the life-giving liquid to the ground. "Drink, drink, you swine!" he yelled. We knelt and licked the water off the ground while the SS whipped us. Then they ordered us to line up.

I looked ahead and my survival instinct told me to observe that anyone who had a sore, a bandage, a limp, was sent to the left by the flick of Dr. Mengele's finger. I watched as my cousins and friends from Edeleny and Miskolc, young women who just a few months ago were full of vitality, but were now broken and lacked the energy even to walk in the line, were immediately sent to the left. Again, without saying goodbye, my childhood companions were gone. But I had no time to mourn.

I devised a plan, and we agreed that the weakest of us among us, Anyu, would go first in the line for the selection, and Lilli and I would follow. I did not want to be separated from Anyu and from my Aunt Lilli, who felt too burdened by life to struggle by herself. Just seconds before we reached the "Angel of Death," I reached down and tore the paper bandages off my mother's legs and hit her on the back, which straightened her up, momentarily. She quickened her steps, and, as I held my breath, she miraculously passed. Lilli and I followed. I looked up to heaven and murmured a silent prayer.

Those of us who were left were all taken to the showers. My cousin Miriam did not want to go in.

"It is a trap!" she screamed. "They want to trick us and kill us like they have done to the others."

For a few minutes I thought of my grandparents, my aunts, and my cousins, but I chased away the image of their deaths.

"Maybe they did kill many, but I know that Grandma and Grandpa and the rest of the family are still alive, somewhere around here, and we'll see them soon," I said, and embraced the wasted body of my mother, who looked at me with questioning eyes.

After the showers, we were left outside, naked, shivering in the cold Silesian night for hours before we were herded into a large, empty building, where we fell on each other in exhaustion. The single, bare light bulb, again, high up near the ceiling, shed a weak, dull light upon our unclothed bodies. The image of a bare light bulb hanging on a wire remained with me throughout the years as the symbol of naked bodies, hairless heads, exposed cruelty, and unconcealed death.

The next morning we were lined up to have our heads shaven again. As I bent down, I felt such desperation as if my head would be chopped off, not just my hair. Somehow the little bit of hair that grew out during the summer in Plasow made me feel more protected, more normal. Being shaven again brought into focus my utter helplessness, my total lack of control. Finally, in the next line, we received some clothing. Following that our left arms were tattooed. I looked at the woman's tattooing hand with some detachment as the numbers A-18273 appeared on my left arm, and thought how this number will, from now on, represent my identity. We assumed that being tattooed was a good sign and hoped that we would be saved for working camp again.

Our wooden barrack was #20 in the BIIc *Lager*, one of many that lined up on the two sides of the road. Our lager was separated from the adjacent ones by an electric fence. Next to the fence was a ditch where those who were killed or died that day, either by touching the electric fence or in other ways, were thrown in; their bodies remained there until the truck came to pick them up and take them away.

Inside the barrack there were two rows of wooden platforms, maybe 20 on each side. Each platform had three levels; ten inmates were assigned to each level. It was almost impossible to turn when we finally squeezed ourselves up on the board. But when the weather became cold, and since we had no blankets, we welcomed each other's warm bodies. The rows of platforms were separated in the middle of the barrack by an elevated brick walkway where the *Blockaltaste*, a Polish Jewish woman, a "veteran" of Auschwitz, would march up and down to supervise us and wake us up at dawn by poking us with a long pole. Years later, when we visited Auschwitz, I had to touch the wooden planks to convince myself that I was really there once. The carvings of names in the wood by the prisoners testified also that once we occupied those hard wooden planks.

Anyu continued to have a fever every afternoon. In the evenings she became cold, her body was shaking, her teeth were chattering. Sometimes I would lie on top of her to give her some warmth. Still, in the morning she would recover and was able to stand in *Zahl-Appel*, when the camp commandant rode in on his white horse to count the inmates. The *Zahl-Appel* occurred twice a day, morning and evening; we stood in row after row for hours, motionless, until his arrival. If someone couldn't stand any longer, she was made to kneel or was beaten.

One night Lilli developed severe diarrhea and rushed to the latrines. She was squatting over the hole when somehow she lost her balance and fell in. She was lucky that there were other women there, who pulled her out, dragged her to the washroom and cleaned her up. But she could no longer use her dress and she came back to our barrack, cold and nude but grateful she didn't drown in the excrement. We pulled her up on the plank, warmed her and she fell asleep, exhausted. We realized hours later when we were awakened that she had no clothes to put on. Someone, miraculously, produced something like a large paper bag that used to contain dry cement and we wrapped her in it and pushed her out the door, just in time to stand in line. But she couldn't escape the watchful eyes of the commandant as he passed us, counting. He shouted down from his horse to remove the bag, and two guards yanked at the cover and exposed her. She stood there, frozen, like the Pillar of Salt in the biblical story of Lot's wife, until the beating she received left her bleeding and she collapsed. She was carried inside, and we stayed on our knees for the rest of the day as punishment.

The Nazis were obsessed with keeping us germ free to prevent a major outbreak of disease. They used strong disinfectant everywhere—its noxious odor is still in my nostrils—and sprayed us with pesticides from low-flying airplanes. While others ran inside in panic, I looked at these giant birds with amazement, since I had never seen an airplane so close before, and ignored the danger they presented.

They would also take us regularly to the showers, about once a week. We usually passed by the Nazi officers' housing, which looked like ordinary residences; they could have been anywhere else in the world, with well-tended little gardens, full of beautiful flowers. In front of the houses, near the road, there was a large swimming pool, its clear blue water glistening in the sun, beckoning me to enjoy its magic. It was a hot August afternoon, and I forgot where I was or who I was, and before anyone could stop me, I dashed out of the line and headed straight for the pool. I dove into the sparkling, cool water, swam its length, and emerged, victoriously, at the other end. Had I won an Olympic medal, I could not have felt more accomplished. "Have you gone mad?" I heard Anyu's terrified voice when I caught up with the others, and only then did I realize how I miraculously avoided being shot by the guards and how my reckless bravery could have caused my mother a heart attack, and possibly my death. Looking back at this episode, I think it was not just reckless behavior, but a most basic instinct to be a "normal" teenager, seeking something that was fun and pleasurable. In that sense it contributed to my affirmation of life, combating hopelessness and despair.

At another time while walking back from the showers, I found two treasures: a little aluminum knife, perhaps just a toy, and a thin silver necklace. I quickly hid the knife inside my shoe and put the necklace on my neck. I was sure that the knife would be extremely useful in cutting my bread, or spreading the occasional margarine that we got, but the necklace was the real treasure. Having lost my beloved Lavender Kerchief, the necklace would take its place as something pretty, feminine, something that would represent the other, normal world, in spite of my gray prison garb and my shaven head. My happiness didn't last long, however, because when we met our *Blockalteste* at the barrack, she noticed the chain on my neck.

"Give that to me, immediately" she ordered me sharply. She had a whip in her hand, her voice was threatening, and so I obeyed her without protest. But Anyu couldn't stand my fallen face and she confronted the *Blockalteste* fearlessly:

"You ought to be ashamed of yourself, you, a Jewish daughter. What would your mother say if she saw you taking away a worthless jewel from a young girl who has lost everything she once had?"

The *Blockalteste* was dumbfounded; no prisoner had ever dared to speak to her this way. I was petrified, waiting for the whip to come down on us, but she just stood there, speechless, as if listening to her own mother's voice. Anyu, encouraged by the *Blockalteste*'s silence, continued:

"So keep the chain, but in return give her some extra soup so she won't die of hunger."

The *Blockalteste* did not respond, but from that day on, she ladled a double portion of soup into my bowl.

One day we were marching again to the baths to be disinfected. As we passed a fenced-in area where men were building a road, I suddenly saw my uncle, Erno, among the men. He was Anyu's younger brother, 28 years old, handsome, not yet married. He had been taken away to forced labor camp years before. Even though we tried to help him avoid the Russian front, way back in 1942, in the end he was taken to detention camp, and we did not know his whereabouts until that moment when we found him there in Auschwitz. Our excitement and joy was hard to contain—those in our group who knew him shared in our happiness at seeing him alive. He also saw us, but all he could do was to wave to us. On the way back we looked anxiously to see if he was still there. To our amazement, he was standing near the fence, and when he saw us, in one leap he jumped over the fence, stuck a bread in my mother's hand and a sweater in mine, and embraced us for a few moments, saying, "I'll see you next week." And then he was gone, just as suddenly as he appeared. I still felt his strong arms around me and saw his smiling, encouraging face as we walked back to camp. This, again, made me believe that miracles can happen, and our hopes were rekindled. But the next time we walked down the same road, my uncle was not there, nor was he there ever again. After the war we were told that shortly following our encounter, he was executed; perhaps he was part of the *Sondercommando*, a unit of prisoners who worked in the gas chambers and who were always eliminated after three months of "service." [I continue to search through the International Red Cross, to find out how he perished, but so far I have received no information about his death.]

The days were getting shorter and we were in the Hebrew month of *Elul*, the month before the Jewish New Year. Day after day the sirens wailed, warning

67

the Nazis of yet another air attack by the Allies, and we were hoping, with trepidation, for our liberation. While the Germans were hiding in their shelters, we stood outside, watching the planes go by without dropping their bombs on us. I felt that, while the bombs could kill us, we could also be liberated. I was convinced that the sirens were substitutes for the sounds of the *Shofar*, the ram's horn that is sounded every day in the month of *Elul* in synagogues all over the world, and that it was meant to awaken our enemies to their wrong-doings, and it was a signal for our deliverance. It seemed logical to me that even though God would send this message to us through the instrument of war, those who believed in Him could easily recognize it. Only a few girls argued with me. "You are so foolish, so naïve," said Olga from my aunt's generation. But Anyu said I was right, and the doubter was silenced. I held fast on to my belief and ignored the flames of the chimneys.

OUR "DOMESTIC LIFE" — Wiesau

It was the eve of our Rosh Hashanah holiday when the announcement came at the morning *Zahl-Appel* that ordered us to march to the baths. Going to the baths would generally create fear; this time, however, we stayed calm even when told to get undressed and get into the showers. We were hoping that we would be taken to another working camp, another life-extension.

We received newly disinfected clothes, discards from recently murdered "sisters." Mine must have been from someone who was my size; perhaps she was a bit older than I. I thought, yes, this must have been her Shabbat dress. It was a brown tweed fabric, in good condition. Maybe she just got it for her birthday and never even had a chance to wear it. Maybe she had brought it along in her knapsack, something very precious to her, the way I had carried my lavender kerchief with me until it also ended up in the heap of shed garments.

"Stop daydreaming and hurry on!" Anyu's worried voice intruded into my thoughts. "Now we just have to be sure that we stay together." The ever-nagging anxiety grabbed my stomach as we pushed ourselves ahead and boarded the train. Again, we had no idea where we were heading or what awaited us when we got there.

Hours later we arrived at WIESAU, as the sign informed us at the station. A few among us calculated that we were farther away from the Russian border, and, indeed, we no longer heard the sound of the guns from the Eastern front. Our chance for liberation was diminished. Some women who were familiar with the area said that we were northwest of Auschwitz, near the Silesian City of Bunzlau. The nearest big city was Breslau.

We arrived at the camp as the sun was sending its orange rays over the hills. It was a small camp; the barracks formed a U-shape with a square in the middle. The camp held only about five hundred prisoners, and because of its small size, neat physical arrangement, and the exceptionally humane reception by the camp commandant, we were euphoric. We stood at attention, all five hundred of us, all women, and listened to the camp commandant who stood on an elevation giving us a Rosh Hashanah "sermon."

"You work hard, obey the rules, and everything will be all right. In honor of your holiday tomorrow, you don't have to go to work. Happy New Year."

We looked at each other, confounded. Could this be real, we asked each other, or was it a trick to lure us into something dangerous and cruel?

"Just enjoy our good fortune," said Fradi, my third cousin. So we entered our barracks where there was another surprise: regular bunk beds, not just wooden slabs, and there was a blanket for each person, and a wooden table with benches in the middle of the room. There was a washroom a few barracks away. The camp kitchen was nearby and behind it the garbage dump, the site of future "treasure hunts." There was even an infirmary in one of the middle barracks, and we were told that if anyone needed medical attention, they should go there. Of course, we knew better than to go near any "medical" facility, the place from where people could be taken away and sent to the gas chamber.

We gathered the next day in small groups and together we chanted the holiday prayers. Most of us knew the important ones by heart; they brought back memories of home, of parents and grandparents, of special foods—the apple dipped in honey—and our hearts were filled with sadness but also with gratitude for our present good luck. The face of Judy, my best friend, kept intruding into my thoughts; she didn't even try to struggle—she just quit. We talked about our friends and cousins who were sent to the gas chambers after our arrival in Auschwitz the second time, and we fantasized how they could have been saved if they were here with us.

The following day I was in a creative mood. I got up even before the *Zahl-Appel* and decided to "landscape" the front of our barrack. I saw some whitewashed rocks and pebbles behind the kitchen, and I created a Hungarian *Matyo* folk-design, with intricate flowers and leaves that covered several feet of ground and gave our barrack a special look. I was very proud of my work; it made me feel as if I had brought something from home to our lives. But others made fun of it, even reprimanded me for wanting to appear patriotic to the country that had not protected us, and which allowed the Nazis to wipe out most of Hungary's Jewish population. Still, I left it there until the rain washed most of it away.

Our daily work routine was to dig trenches and lay sewer pipes, just outside the camp. We hauled the dirt and rocks in wagons, pushing them or pulling them, always under the watchful eyes of the guards who used their whips and their dogs to make us perform faster. Sometimes I felt that I could not continue any more, but somehow I pushed myself on. As the weather turned colder, the ground froze and the work became even harder.

One Saturday six women who came from rabbinical families decided that it was forbidden by the Torah to work on the Shabbat, and therefore refused to participate in the task. These women were older than I, and had some religious authority among us, especially two sisters who owned a small prayer book. I felt angry that instead of twelve of us to push the heavy wagon full of pipes, now there would only be six, and I could barely keep up with the twelve. But I also acknowledged that they were only following what the Torah commanded us. I knew that the day of Shabbat was holy, and I recited the fourth commandment that I learned by heart in my Hebrew class: "…but on the seventh day you shall not do any work, you, your son, your daughter, your male or female slaves…" What to do, who was right? What should I do? I didn't have much time to ponder because the *Kapo* appeared and saw the six women not working and severely beat them with his whip. The enemy resolved our religious dilemma.

Sometime in November Anyu's cousin, Mintsu, who was in her eighth month of pregnancy, was sent to the infirmary by the *Blockalteste*. She assured us that Mintsu would be taken to a hospital, not far from the camp, where she would deliver her baby, and then be sent back to us. We were always protecting Mintsu after she miraculously avoided selection in Auschwitz, hoping that she would be able to have the baby in the camp, as promised by the commandant when we had first arrived. The truck came the next day, and they loaded up all the sick women from the camp infirmary, including Mintsu, who smiled at us reassuringly as she waved goodbye. The truck took them to Gross-Rosen, another major camp near Breslau. But our hopes were again crushed—she never returned to us, and we never heard from her again. We found out later through the grapevine that everyone who was taken away on that day was killed there.

Anyu was too weak to perform the heavy work we were assigned to do because she was still suffering from the malaria-like fever that returned every afternoon, and she had no appetite. I refused to take her to the infirmary, fearing that they would not let her out. On days when my mother was especially weak, I would find places to hide her before we left for work, sometimes in the latrines, sometimes in the barrack, and sometimes in the garbage heap next to the kitchen. I was familiar with the garbage dump because I used to go there to look for food scraps and potato peels, until one day a truck dumped a new load of garbage on top of me, and in the midst of this bounty, I almost suffocated. But I was desperate, and when no other safe place was found, I hid her there. After we returned from work I would drag her out of the garbage or find her at the other hiding places. My cousins helped me in this dangerous game, and each time we found her, I gave thanks to God for saving her.

Anyu was willing to listen to me and do what I instructed—quite the opposite of what our relationship was before when she was the one who always dictated to me what to do. But she didn't give up the appearance of being in charge, and, unconsciously, I supported her in that. Perhaps I felt safer if I could look at her as someone who still has some control over our lives.

I made friends with one of the Wehrmacht guards who watched us as we pushed the loaded wagons in the howling wind and knee-deep snow that piled up on the opposite sides of the train tracks. He was a man of small stature, very old, wearing a loose-fitting uniform; most of his teeth were missing. He was not very menacing, although he walked around with a gun on his shoulder. He liked me in a grandfatherly way and, occasionally, let me take a break when I felt I could not go on. One day I asked him if he could get me an onion because Anyu had no appetite and would not eat no matter how I begged or cajoled her. I was desperate—I knew that if she didn't eat, she would die in a few days. I also knew that I could not hide her forever, and eventually they would discover her and take her away. Perhaps because I reminded him of his own granddaughter, the next day the old guard pushed an onion into my hand. That evening I sneaked into the boiler room, and I held a slice of bread against the flames to toast it. Then I smeared it with the onion. I ran back to the barrack to give her the bread while it was still warm. She took a bite, the first in days, and I sighed with relief and gratitude toward the old German "grandfather" guard.

When my mother got a little bit stronger, she was able to get into the *Schalerei*, in the kitchen where they peeled the potatoes. After work she would come back to the barrack with potato peels hidden in the bosom of her dress. We had the raw potato peel for desert, and how delicious it tasted when occasionally we were able to roast it. On some lucky days my mother and her cousin Elza were sent out to the fields to dig up potatoes for the German kitchen. On those days they stuffed a few into their dresses, and if they avoided the sharp eyes of the guards, we had an extra treat that evening.

When it started to snow, we got some flimsy coats, but mine was short and my legs were still very cold. I had also acquired an extra pair of underwear and my creative mother had an idea. Somehow she got hold of a needle and thread, and she made pants out of my brown underwear and the bottom part of my dress. It certainly did not look like a Parisian design, but when I put it on, I curtsied and twirled around to the admiring looks of everyone in the barrack. The next day I felt much warmer and more protected.

Lilli, who had just turned 23 the previous summer, had been unhappy because she was housed in a different barrack, and felt isolated and neglected by us. She even reproached my mother, saying, "You only worry about Erika, and don't even try to help me when you know that five women who were weak were taken away already from my barrack, and we don't know what happened to them. What if I get sick? How will you know?"

My mother became angry because she felt she was being unjustly accused, and harsh words were exchanged. I crouched on top of the bunk so that my presence would cause no further irritation between them. I wanted to reassure

Lilli that I would share my mother with her even if in reality I could not get her into our barrack. Lilli had always felt that she was not as important to her own mother as her older siblings were. She was the eleventh child of my grandmother, having only one younger brother, and she had not gotten much attention. The other girls in the room listened, perhaps each feeling a little bit more abandoned by their own mothers, perhaps envious of my good fortune. And I just wanted to hide.

Because of the small size of the camp and the freedom to move around and communicate with each other, a kind of "domestic" atmosphere developed. It was as if someone had given permission to exhibit familial competition, to express feelings of hurt and anger, as well as affection, in the relationships among us. It appeared that the initial reaction of shock and numbness to the suffering and pain changed into more "ordinary" emotional reactions to the situation.

By the middle of December the ground froze. A few feet of snow covered all the trenches, the road, and the hills, and all work had to stop. We hadn't seen our benevolent commandant for several weeks—he disappeared like a mirage. It was rumored that he was removed from his post because he was too good, and we realized that our stay in Wiesau, which was considerably better than in the other camps, was coming to an end. Our hopes about the Soviets freeing us also vanished. When the order came to transfer us to another camp, we no longer had the spirit to find a good omen in the change. We were disheartened and gloomy. The train came, and we climbed aboard, our daily bread ration in our hands. We huddled together on the floor, our bodies seeking the warmth of each other, resigned that our slavery had not ended.

❧

"THE SLAP" — Reichenbach

The train was moving slowly. I looked out through the narrow window and saw a beautiful landscape of mountains and fields, all frozen and covered with sparkling white snow. Then the train passed through bombed-out cities and ruined towns; the snow could not cover their ugliness and devastation. Again this feeling of sadness came upon me, but back somewhere in my mind a voice was telling me, "Rejoice in the ruination of your enemy because that will be your salvation." I kept my thoughts and feelings to myself.

When we arrived the next day, the sign on the railroad station read REICHENBACH. Some women thought that they had heard about the place, that it was an industrial town, somewhere in Upper Silesia. We scrambled out of the train, straightening our aching bodies, and automatically lined up in rows of five even before the order came. We walked on the snowy road several miles before we arrived at the camp.

The barracks were made of stone bricks. There were windows on one side of the barrack, but they had no glass, just gaping holes, offering unobstructed entrance for the howling wind and blowing snow. My mother and I found two spaces next to each other on the cold and slippery cement floor and we spread a thin layer of straw, arranging it carefully so that it would cover the floor evenly, neither of us having it thinner or heavier than the other. We even got one blanket, made of rough, gray material, something that was used for horses. We were exhausted from the train ride from Wiesau and the long walk after that. Rumor had it that here in Reichenbach we would be working in an airplane factory, indoors, safe from the elements. I wanted to feel hopeful that the work at this place would be better than the last one, that our food would improve, and that we wouldn't get sick so much from the backbreaking work in the frozen hills.

I lay down like a log with Anyu next to me, spreading the blanket over the two of us though it was not wide enough to cover us both. I shivered from the cold and had a hard time falling asleep. I felt the cold seeping through the straw under me, entering my body, occupying it like a foreign force. The wind swept over my head, which I tried to bury under the blanket. I was thinking of my bed at home, in Miskolc, its down comforter that I had to share with my cousin who had come to live with us so she could go to school. I had often complained to my mother about not having my own bed, but she paid no attention to me since it was natural for us to share our beds with relatives whenever it was necessary.

The snow was blowing through the window, and we were next to the opening. Suddenly, my mother got up and shook the snow off the blanket and then instead of covering both of us again, she just spread it over me and tried to tuck me in. I tore the blanket off and jumped up and insisted that we both get under it. It soon became a tug of war—I was pushing my mother down, she was pushing me away, the blanket tangled under our feet.

"Be quiet, you, two, you don't let us sleep," the women around us complained angrily about our struggle, unaware of what the fuss was all about. I was determined that I was not going to let my mother freeze while I was wrapped cozily in the blanket. And then, like a lightening, I felt the sting of a slap on my face. My mother had never slapped me before. This was such a shock to me, I was stunned, and my throat closed up. She looked at me with a stern expression, the kind I knew from my early years that she meant business. She said, "You must obey me. It's written in the Ten Commandments. A mother knows better what is good for both of us. I want no arguments."

The woman next to us propped her head on her elbow and said loudly: "Good, she deserved it. Now at least you'll be quiet and we can go to sleep."

Defeated, I curled up on the floor, turned away from Anyu, but still felt her back against mine. I pulled the scratchy blanket over my stinging face, confused about the order of the world, about a child's duty to her parent, and about how any God could order me to let my mother freeze. I fell asleep and dreamed of horses being cold in a stable, and I was trying to cover them with their blankets but I was too short to reach them.

MY MOTHER GREW — Reichenbach–Langenbielau

The pipes in the washroom were frozen solid. Our whole world was frozen. It was dark, the middle of winter, most of the camp was still asleep, not ready to awaken from their nightmares and face another day. On the way to the latrines, I gathered some snow in a can, and in the latrines I washed myself before anyone woke up; this way I had some privacy. I was alone with my body. "You'll surely get pneumonia," warned Anyu, but she couldn't keep me from performing my bath ritual whenever I could.

As I was rubbing my body, I remembered longingly when I was a little girl in Hungary, how we used to take our baths in the kitchen, one by one, in a barrel filled with warm water from the big pot on the stove. I always worried that someone would walk in on me when I was naked and wanted to get out as fast as I could. Later, when they remodeled our apartment, they made a bathroom, which had a tub and a water heater, and the door could be closed though not locked. I would spend a long time in there as the water was being heated, standing close to the tank, spreading my arms around it and hugging it as if it were a person with a warm body. To my embarrassment, I was once discovered by our maid, who made fun of me, and after that I stopped doing it.

Every morning the march to the work place in Langenbielau took about an hour. It was still dark when we left the camp in Reichenbach; the long line of inmates curved along the road like a black snake against the whiteness of the glistening snow. Many guards, armed with guns and dogs, always accompanied the group. If a prisoner fell either from weakness or because she lost her balance, she would be first ordered to get up, and if she couldn't, guards would set the dogs on her. If that didn't work, she would be shot and the group would continue walking. No one was allowed to look back. Sometimes we found frozen bodies on the side of the road that were not picked up from days earlier.

We always marched, five in a row, row after row, slipping and sliding precariously on the frozen ball of snow that accumulated under our wooden-platform shoes. In our row was my mother, me, Lilli, Frimet, the rabbi's daughter from Edeleny, and Vali, a distant cousin. We had agreed that the weakest one would be always in the middle, so if she couldn't walk, we could carry her for a while. My Aunt Lilli had become depressed and despondent since we left Wiesau and had little desire to carry herself. Frimet and Vali supported her faithfully, and Frimet was especially able to urge Lilli to go on, to try harder. Anyu would get impatient with her and would admonish her for giving up too easily. My mother could not tolerate weakness; she could never acknowledge her own fear or anxiety—these feelings were life threatening there.

My mother also had another distant cousin with us, Elza. Elza had her two daughters with her, Fradi and Miriam. There was a close bond between Elza and her older daughter Fradi, but Miriam often felt left out. She thought that they always had secrets to hide, things to share. In the camps the competition for mothers became more acute.

"You always take care of Fradi first, even here. You don't really love me," Miriam reproached her mother. "I wish my father were here—he would be on my side."

Such outbursts were usually followed by an angry response from Elza, which made Miriam feel more rejected, evoking from her mother the very thing she was afraid of. Miriam had a generally pessimistic outlook on life. She always expected the worst, which made her life in the camps even more unbearable. When I told her to look at the sun that was trying to come out from behind the clouds, she would say that it's no use, the clouds will cover it again.

When Miriam became weaker, and had a difficult time maintaining her balance because of the accumulated snowballs under her shoes, we put her in the middle of our row, and Vali and I held on to her and steadied her.

"I can't, I just can't," she cried. "It's better if you just leave me on the side of the road. Let them shoot me."

I held on to her more tightly and started humming a melody that her father used to sing on Shabbat afternoons when I visited them in Miskolc.

"You remember how we used to sit in the dark, before Shabbat had ended—that special time of the day when the sun had already gone down on the horizon, but the three stars had not yet appeared in the sky—singing, swaying to the melancholy melody, saying *"Gott Fun Avrohom,"* saying goodbye to the holy day?"

The thought of Miriam's close relationship with her father, remembering the special time together, revived her spirit and she went on. Still the walking became more and more difficult until a new idea occurred to me.

"Hey, let's pretend that we are on the ice-skating rink on the shimmering surface of the lake, and there is this beautiful music, and we just learned how to do that fancy footwork, and we are both trying to win a prize."

Pretty soon Miriam joined me in the fantasy. I kept humming the music, instructing her on the technique, trying to laugh as I caught her when she started to fall.

At home Miriam's very religious father did not allow her to ice-skate because there were boys at the skating place, and skating wasn't a modest behavior. I, on the other hand, thanks to Anyu's intervention with our rabbi, had been permitted. Skating had strengthened my legs, and I had to do a lot of exercises since the hip surgery in my early childhood.

But Miriam was a worrier. No matter how much I tried to show her a different outlook on life, she was stuck in her old groove, and I couldn't dislodge her. One day we both received an extra pair of underwear, and I immediately put them on to keep me warmer. Not Miriam. "I'll save it for when it gets even colder. You always have to have something in reserve," she said apprehensively.

"That's the way I also used to be," I said and imagined my parents talking to me, saying, "Save the Shabbat dress, don't wear your new shoes, eat only half an orange, save the other half for a snack." I heard my parents' voices echoing in my head.

"Watch for that furniture, don't jump on it, it will have to stay nice for the time when you're a big girl and your future husband comes to see you."

I still saw Apu's face as he gently admonished me when I acted wild. I suddenly felt anger rising in my chest as I wondered whether I would ever sit on that carefully preserved couch again. Why did I have to be so careful, why did we have to save things for a tomorrow that would never come? But underneath my anger I sensed my increasing foreboding, not about the loss of our furniture, but about never hearing my father's voice again.

Three days later Miriam was taken to the hospital with pneumonia.

From early morning until evening, we worked in the Farben airplane factory in Langenbielau. We were happy to be inside, out of the wind and snow. It was a very large plant, with many divisions, and at first our little group was assigned to a small room. There we sat around a long table and were taught by an old German *Arbeitsfuhrer*, or work-supervisor, how to grind, sand, and polish parts of the instruments, which, after they were tested, would be installed in airplanes. The room was called the *Schleiferei*, which meant the polishing place. It was very delicate work, and Anyu was given the task of testing each piece by applying pressure with a machine that would show if the polished parts fit together perfectly. If they didn't fit, she had to give them back to us to redo the work with precision and speed.

The old man was the technical expert and supervised our work. He was a tall, thin man, with a gaunt, colorless face that blended in with his drab, civilian-gray suit. He wore a somber, even sad expression. The SS guard was especially vicious there, and even the supervisor was careful to avoid attracting the ire of the guard. How surprised we were when one day he gave Anyu a kerchief to cover her bare head. Then he reached into his pocket and pulled out a red apple and quickly handed it to me. I was shocked, looked at him with amazement, and then quickly hid the apple on my lap. It seemed to me that his face had changed: there was a benign look in his eyes, even a faint smile on his lips. He could be my grandfather, I thought, probably missing his granddaughter who was far away. Any old man at that time looked like a grandfather to me. I grabbed his hand and I kissed it, something I would have done to my own grandfather. At lunchtime I cut the apple into 22 pieces, gave everyone a piece, and we recited the blessing for a new fruit. We figured that that day was *Tu B'Shvat*, the New Year of the Trees, when it was customary for the Jews in Hungary to eat a new fruit, to celebrate the gift of the trees.

After having been trained by the expert, we were transferred to the main room of the factory. This was a very large hall, with cement walls and floors, full of machinery. Groups of prisoners were working on high stools around long tables, bare lamps overhead. Our group was assigned a place where we were constantly exposed to the watchful eyes of the guards. From the time we arrived at seven in the morning until seven in the evening, we had to stay at our station, except for a short lunch break. We were not allowed to get up to use the toilet, to drink water, to talk or socialize with each other. The SS woman beat us if we could no longer hold ourselves back and urinated on the floor. Some girls managed to "organize" some tin cans, which we kept under the table and used to relieve ourselves.

My mother, who again was given the task of testing the assembled parts, carried a great responsibility, and everything had to go through her watchful eyes and swift fingers until the final inspection by another *Arbeitsfuhrer*, a civilian Nazi, who watched us carefully. The uniformed guards made sure that we did not talk or get up from the table.

At one point I looked at Anyu, and suddenly realized that between the rounds of the supervisor, she let through pieces that did not withstand the test. I continued doing my work but I felt my bowels cramped, and I needed to go to the toilet very badly but knew I couldn't. How could she do this? I asked myself. Why is she risking her life and the lives of the rest us? This would bring certain punishment, even death, if they caught her. Was she aware of what she was doing or had she lost her skill or her mind? I struggled with my thoughts while I looked at my mother's calm face, which did not betray anything. I was prepared for the worst. I knew that if she was noticed, she would be shot for sabotage and probably the whole group would be held responsible. I felt I had to do something—I had to avert the attention of the *Arbeitsfuhrer* so she wouldn't be caught. I decided that I would take my chances and get the empty can from under the table, move to the other end of the table and relieve myself.

"You dirty swine!" barked the SS, and the guard's whip came down on me immediately. I was knocked over by its violence, but I did not feel the pain—I was on a mission and I felt I had won. The commotion I created drew attention to me, and away from my mother.

Finally, the day came to an end, and we started our march back to the camp. We were trudging through the snow, walking silently, as if this had been just another ordinary day. Finally I could no longer contain myself, and I asked:

"Why did you do it?"

Anyu answered, casually: "At least I can slow down their war a bit. Maybe that airplane will malfunction and it will explode, and we'll have a few less Nazis."

I looked at my mother, and I was sure that I saw her grow several inches. I ignored the fact that she had just put us, and herself, in extreme danger. In my eyes she was a hero.

⚮

Erika Jacoby

THE SHABBAT "MANNA" — Langenbielau

The winter of 1945 dragged on. We spent endless hours fantasizing about food, devising elaborate recipes and sumptuous feasts on our long daily marches to and from the factory. But our stomachs became more and more demanding. We all tried to figure out how to "organize" some extra food; "organizing" meant to get hold of, by manipulating or stealing. I was too scared of being beaten if caught stealing from the kitchen, so most often I relied on my good luck or careful planning. We tried to figure out where to stand in line when they were giving out the soup. Usually the end of the line was the best, because the bottom of the kettle was thicker and more filling. But sometimes this backfired, because they often ran out of soup by the time we got there, and then we had only our daily slice of bread to quiet our grumbling stomachs. One day my mother and I reached the SS woman who was dishing out the soup, and to our distress, we both received only half a portion since we were at the end of the line.

That afternoon an air raid resulted in general confusion at the plant. Some groups were led to a different part of the factory, while we stayed locked in the yard, guarded by vicious dogs watching us so we wouldn't escape. The SS jammed into the shelter. We stood in the yard and watched with fascination as the airplanes zoomed by. Then there was a giant explosion—one bomb hit the part of the structure that was supposed to be the safest, and many prisoners were killed. Finally the sirens sounded again, signaling the end of the raid. I was surprised at how shaken I felt. It was difficult for me to cope with the onslaught of disparate feelings: terror of almost dying in the attack, joy that the Allies had hit their target, and crushing sorrow over the deaths of my fellow inmates.

We couldn't get back to our workplace that afternoon, and all the inmates who survived were crowded into the yard, men and women together. Then we saw a group of men trying to get through the mob of people. These men all wore the prisoners' garb, but somehow they looked better fed, more "civilized" than we. Suddenly, one tall handsome man appeared in front of me, looked at me, and handed me a pot with a handle and a cover on it, touching my fingers, making sure I held on to it. I looked up and saw him smile. I was so surprised that I did not even have the time to think whether I should take it or not. As quickly as he came, the tall vision disappeared into the crowd. I stood there, dumbfounded, holding the heavy pot, asking everyone:

"Why did he give it to me? Was this his own food? Why did he give it away?"

"Just open it and eat," I was nudged by those around me. "Don't ask so many questions."

I opened the pot, carefully. It was full to the brim with heavy, thick soup, the kind I often fantasized about getting when I was standing in line. Although I was famished, I waited—I wanted to savor the moment as I imagined that the soup had everything in it I always hoped for: fat, white barley, big chunks of all kinds of roots, perhaps even pieces of meat which I did not want to acknowledge, because it was not kosher. I knew that it was much more than I could eat by myself. I knew I couldn't hide the soup; I knew everybody was hungry, and I was exceptionally lucky to get it, but I really didn't feel that I deserved it. Still, I also felt that somehow God took care of me because I didn't get my full portion of soup earlier. My faith in God was strengthened, again. Maybe I was worthy of God's protection and care, I thought.

"Here, you give everyone some," I told Frimet, the rabbi's daughter, after a few moments of hesitation. I trusted her most, more than myself, that she would distribute the treasured gift fairly to our little group.

Even with the pitiful portions of daily bread we received, Anyu and I used to break off part of the bread, or would share one slice between the two of us, every day, and tucked the rest away, saving it for Shabbat. The tradition back home was to have two loaves of *chalah* (twisted bread) for Shabbat, the way the Israelites were given a double portion of the *Manna* on Shabbat when they wandered in the desert. So we started preparing for Shabbat on Sunday, each day getting us closer to it, each day giving us purpose to go on. I remembered the Hebrew saying, "Whoever prepares on the eve of Shabbat will eat on the Shabbat…" I also recalled the tale of the ant and the grasshopper, a lesson that was so ingrained into our minds by our parents and teachers.

"Be responsible, make plans, don't waste, then you will have control over your life." These words may have lost their meaning here, but we tried, desperately, to find ways to prove that everything was not negated. This purposefulness and the belief that we acted in accordance with the teaching of our heritage gave us extra strength, despite the horrors and degradation of our everyday life. So we saved our morsels every day.

"They stole our bread!" cried Anyu one day. "Someone found our hiding place and stole our bread." Her face became hard, and I could see how she tried to control herself.

"It couldn't be," I argued. "Who would take our bread? Surely, everyone knows that we were saving it for Shabbat. No, no, it can't be, you must have lost it somewhere," and my tears flowed.

"You are so naïve, daughter. When people are hungry, they do terrible things," said my mother, trying to calm herself and me.

I couldn't stop sobbing. Just a few weeks before, someone had unselfishly given me a pot of soup. Before that there were two instances when my enemy, first the German guard and then the German work supervisor, had gifted me with an onion and then an apple. I felt so confused. I felt cheated by my fellow inmates who were all victims like me. Nothing was clear any more. We didn't just lose the precious bread, but more than that—my faith in my fellow human beings was so terribly shaken.

Because of the constant hunger and our diminishing physical strength, I had to find some way to supplement our daily diet. One day the opportunity presented itself, and I found a way to improve our situation a bit. It became my habit that at our lunchtime, or whenever I could, I would play with the tools and the scrap metal and the colored wiring that I worked with, which was lying around. It kept away my boredom and fatigue and gave me a little excitement. I twisted the wires with the pliers, filed the metal into shapes, creating little toys and jewelry. I liked what I made, and from then on I progressed to make charms, pins, bracelets. My friends kept a lookout and quickly informed me when an SS was coming by. One day, however, I was caught by one of the Wehrmacht soldiers.

"What are you hiding there?" he demanded. "Show me what you have there."

Anxiously, I pulled out the toys from inside my blouse where I had hidden them, and lined them up on the table. There they stood, the sled, the violin, the pin in the shape of a heart, the miniature dolls holding hands.

"I like these. Give them to me, and make some more so I can send them home to my children," said the soldier.

I sighed with relief—he didn't punish me. He wanted a favor from me, he, the powerful, from me, the weak one. I didn't want to part with my "toys," but I had no choice. I wondered how many children he had, how old they were. I started to look at him as a person, not just as someone who had total control over me. Emboldened, I said, hesitantly:

"Please, give me some extra food, and I'll make some more." To my amazement he reached into his pocket and took out some biscuits.

"Just keep it for yourself—let no one see it," and from then on he rewarded me with something to eat every time I made him something.

Following that, my craft became known even to the SS and to the work supervisors as well as to the more "affluent" inmates, and they gave me orders, which I filled as fast as I could. My hunger was somewhat lessened, and I even put away some food for Shabbat, to have our double portion.

WHEN THE MESSIAH COMES —
Langenbielau, Winter–Spring

Toward the end of the winter, when the days became longer and there was a hint of thaw in the air, I was suddenly transferred to another room to work with a different type of equipment. I was the only girl who was selected for this, and I was the only female to work with a group of men. Anyu became very worried because we couldn't figure out why I was removed from my group and placed far away from the others. Was this a reward or a punishment?

"You always fooled around with your jewelry, and the guard who ordered some for his children didn't want to be found out," said the rabbi's daughter, Frimet, who continued to look at the dark side of events. She was older and more experienced about life, but still, I would rather listen to my cousin, Fradi, who said with a touch of envy in her voice:

"It is because you are so skilled with your hands that they selected you. I wish I could go with you; surely you will have a better place than here, and you might even get more food."

I really had no say in the matter, so the next morning I parted from my mother with much trepidation and headed to the other section of the factory. I took my assigned seat on one side of the table. I didn't dare look around or talk to anyone. The supervisor was standing right next to me, showing me what to do. I felt tense, almost immobilized, afraid that I might not understand his instructions or that I would make a mistake and would be accused of sabotage.

As time went on, I relaxed and started to interact with my co-workers who were mostly older Polish Jewish men, some perhaps my father's age. They didn't understand why I came to work there either. They might even have thought that I was spying on them, and at first they looked at me with some suspicion. But slowly they warmed up to me, and I became their "special girl." I think I represented their collective sisters, daughters, or girlfriends. Often they found little gifts for me. One day a younger man made a comb for me from the metal we worked with.

"Here, now you have some hair, you can comb it and make yourself pretty."

I blushed and could hardly thank him. How could I make myself pretty in the rags that I wore to cover my bones, without soap and water to clean my body? But still I was overjoyed by his gift, and I gladly shared it back in the barrack with my envious cousin.

I enjoyed talking to these men. The supervision was more relaxed, so having a conversation across the table was possible. We had serious discussions about philosophy, religion, literature, but not family; that we avoided, as it caused too much anxiety. This was the first time in my life that adults paid attention to what I thought. I felt important, someone worthy of being listened to, a new view of myself. One man, Aronowitz, must have been a teacher once because he spent a lot of time explaining to me the "real life," the historical background that led to the war. But we often argued about our future. The men were getting underground news about the war situation, and Aronowitz was convinced that the Germans would do away with us before the Soviets could reach us.

"Only if the Russian army advanced faster and by surprise could occupy the town, or if the Americans would bomb the German Headquarters and kill all its leaders and generals, could we be saved," insisted Aronowitz.

"Not so," I said. "It is God who is going to liberate us by sending the Messiah who will save us." He laughed at my naiveté, as he and the others made fun of me.

"So how is it going to be when the Messiah comes, and what do we have to do to hasten his coming?" the men asked me every day and I repeated again and again:

"You have to pray, have faith in God, and be good to each other."

They were amused and laughed but would not let a day go by when they didn't ask me to repeat what I said, again and again.

"You'll see, that's how it will happen—the Messiah will come, I know. My grandfather always told me that when things get very bad, it heralds the coming of the Messiah." I felt absolutely secure in my conviction.

Erika Jacoby

PASSOVER, SPRING, 1945 — Langenbielau

S ometime early in the spring, our camp was transferred to a new place, in the town of Langenbielau, where the factory was located. It was ironic that during the terrible winter storms, we had to walk miles to get to work, and now, with the milder weather, we had to walk only a short distance every day. I felt cheated that I could not see the greening of the fields and the blossoming of the trees on the way.

The new camp was bare—nature had not been allowed to enter. However, the barracks looked less severe; they were made of wood instead of stone blocks. Inside we had bunks to sleep on instead of the cement floor. I climbed up to the top bunk, and Anyu occupied the one under me. Finally I had my own space, I thought, but at first I couldn't relax; I kept looking down to see if she was there. I was used to having her next to me, her body warming mine in the coldness of the night. She reached up to touch me, and finally we fell asleep holding hands.

We could look over the fence and see the men's camp and the SS housing. Some of the more attractive girls were taken by the SS to be their girlfriends. These girls were mostly from Poland and Czechoslovakia with many years of incarceration, but as a result of receiving more food, dresses that fit them, and because their hair was longer, they no longer looked like prisoners but more like the "regular" girls used to look back home. I wondered, with some anxiety, what I would have done if the Germans chose me, but then the thought quickly changed into the clarifying and comforting reality—they would not want a girl who looked like a bony scarecrow, with only a little hair and wearing rags. But spring was in the air and a general restlessness was among us. Toby, a beautiful 18-year-old girl, and a Jewish *Kapo* were caught behind the barracks and were shot. Death was always with us, but being killed while in a loving embrace jolted us. It was a bad omen for a bloody spring.

We had kept close account of the Jewish calendar, and we were pretty accurate. We figured out when Passover would be, and when the day arrived, we planned to hold a Seder in the barrack that night. The evening came, and one of us stood near the door to watch for the approach of any of the guards or *Kapos*. Then we all sat on top of our bunks and started the ceremony. We had no *maror* (bitter herb)—only bitterness. We had no bread, leavened or unleavened (*matza*), but as our tears fell, remembering our lost homes and families, we at least had salt water. We knew the parts of the *Haggadah*, the *Seder* story, by heart, and we started by singing the Four Questions: "*Mah Nishtana Halayla Hazeh*"— "Why is this night different from all other nights?" The question that used to be asked by the youngest child in the family now seemed almost comical, bizarre. We could not sing the answer to the question, *Avadim Hayinu, Ata B'ney Horim*," "We were slaves and now we are free," so we had just skipped it. But when we came to "*Dayenu*," with great effort we each searched for something that we could be thankful for. Some mentioned the fact that they had enough strength and could still work. Vali said that she was glad that the winter was over and she doesn't have to freeze. Anyu was thankful that she had me with her, and I recalled the many mini-miracles that had saved my life. We ended the *Seder* with the traditional singing of "*L'Shana Haba'ah B'Yerushalayim*," "Next Year in Jerusalem," with yearning and hope.

I was determined that I would not eat bread during Passover no matter what. My co-workers tried hard to dissuade me from my crazy clinging to my religious belief, but I would not relent. The men then brought me raw potatoes every day, and sometimes, at great risk, they were able to cook them in the boiler. Anyu and I managed pretty well, but on the sixth and seventh day, we couldn't go to work, so my supply wasn't there. On those days the SS ordered us to stand in *Zahl-Appel*, from morning till evening, the sun beating down on us without relief. We could not figure out why we had to do this, but then most of their orders only served the purpose of making us suffer. Not having eaten anything for two days, I fainted and fell to the ground. Fortunately, only those around me noticed, and they shaded me until I revived. On the eighth day of Passover we went to work again, and I got my daily potato from my friends and one for my mother. Passover ended without my eating bread. I felt very virtuous.

Soon after Passover the air attacks and the mortar gun explosions kept us away from the factory. Now we spent more and more time standing in *Zahl-Appel*, or kneeling as punishment, or just wandering around aimlessly in the camp, weakened by gnawing hunger. There were days when they didn't give us even the meager portions we had gotten earlier. The situation became more tense every day. We often got news from the men through the fence, encouraging us to hold out or to warn us about the SS plan to execute us before we could be liberated.

One day someone pushed a crumpled paper through the fence to me—on it was written "Erika." It was a letter, written by Aronowitz. In it he said:

"We are all praying for our liberation. Don't give up! We will survive, and we'll soon meet in freedom, in the Land of Israel. Your friend, Aronowitz."

I couldn't believe what I read. This man, this non-believer who questioned the value of faith, was now praying for his liberation. I was sure that he wanted me to know that my steady affirmation of the hope for help from heaven had penetrated his consciousness. Perhaps we had, indeed, arrived at messianic times, I thought. I hid the letter in my shoe and took it out and read it over and over that evening and every day after. When we were liberated, I hoped that I could see him; I was sure that he would look for me. But the war ended and Aronowitz disappeared. I asked the men if they knew what happened to him, but no one could give me any information. He might have been among those who were executed before the Nazis left. [I kept the letter for years and searched for him everywhere, even put an ad in the paper in Israel, but I never found him.]

Two days after I received the letter, we were ordered to the back of the camp, near the garbage dump, and commanded to dig our graves. The Nazis cruelly reassured us that they would not allow us to survive and be liberated by the Soviets. We had great difficulty complying with the order because by now we had very little strength left, and we had come to believe that in these last hours of our slavery, they would indeed murder us. Still, in spite of the terror that grabbed my heart, I was able to repeat the *Shma Yisrael,* the prayer that all Jews have said for thousands of years before dying. The guards drove us mercilessly with whips and curses, but we could not finish the task. They allowed us to return to the barracks, but we could not sleep. We felt that although these might be our last hours, we still had to hope that somehow we would escape our death, that the SS would not have enough time to carry out their murderous plan.

Today I often quote someone who said: "I do not believe in miracles; I count on them." I am sure that at that time I did believe in miracles, and unquestioningly I counted on them.

LIBERATION, May 8, 1945 —
I HELD THE SUN IN MY HANDS

We awakened the next morning with the sun shining through the windows. There were no wake-up calls, no guards, no sirens. We cautiously climbed down from our bunks, looked outside, and saw no SS around. Everything was quiet, and an eerie stillness hung in the air. We went outside and slowly approached the gates. The gates were locked but no guards stood outside; gone were the vicious dogs as well. We stood there, stupefied. We couldn't believe our eyes. Was this what we were waiting for? Was this really the end of our slavery? Was this the dawn of our freedom? Or perhaps just a cruel joke, a trick to finish us off quickly? Or perhaps only a dream?

"Let's get out of here!" someone cried, shaking us out of our stupor. I ran behind the dump and got a shovel; others followed me, and we started digging under the electric fence. Gone was the inertia, the weariness that had plagued us all these months. We dug and shoveled, and in a short time we had a hole big enough for me to crawl through since I weighed only about 60 pounds. I carefully slid down into the hole, and, scraping the dirt away on the other side, I pulled myself through.

There I was, standing alone, the fence behind me, facing the wide, open road. I was afraid to take another step and destroy this mirage. Slowly, I started walking forward, looking around to see if someone would shout "Halt!" I turned around and saw the others watching me, mesmerized. Again, I looked around. Not far away I saw the SS headquarters and their living quarters. Everything was deserted. The road was empty, peaceful. In the distance I could see the town—no movement there either. The wind was lightly blowing the brand new leaves on the trees on both sides of the road, gently touching my hollowed cheeks. There were wildflowers in the fields, and the air was clear and fragrant. I looked up at the sky. The sun was now majestically occupying the eastern horizon, sending its rays all around, warming my shrunken body. I stood there, stretching my arms upward, reaching as high as I could. And I held the sun in my hands, as long as I could, praying that it would not fall or disappear.

The others soon followed me, and we approached the city, keeping together, needing each other for support. I wondered if we'd ever be able to walk by ourselves. The streets were abandoned; silence surrounded us. Then we noticed white sheets hanging from the windows, and we wondered if the war was over, and if most of the people in town had run away. We stopped and started to shout, "We are free, we are free!" We cried and we laughed and hugged each other—we felt intoxicated.

Suddenly we heard men singing, and we saw a marching army approaching us. As they got closer, we realized that this was the "Glorious Soviet Liberating Army." They did not look glorious or even well organized. Their march was more like an exhausted procession of men in uniforms who could barely hold up their bodies. Most of them were drunk, singing not in unison but each to his own rhythm. They waved to us, smiling, and we waved back, hesitantly, as if it was our duty to acknowledge their bravery. But we were scared of them and wondered how they would "protect" us. Our fears proved to be well founded, because the officer at the head of the group instructed us to go back to the camp and wait there for further instruction. We did as we were told. Soon their highest officers arrived at the camp, called us to the yard, and told us to stay in the camp, and that we would be assigned to different work sites starting the next day. We were assured that we would be given food.

We went to bed, disappointed, only to be awakened a couple of hours later by hordes of Soviet soldiers entering our barracks, their drunken voices demanding *barishna, barishna*, girls, girls. The Polish inmates in our camp had warned us that these soldiers had been in the army for years and had not seen women for a long time, and they were wild.

And now they wanted girls. The room next to us was hit first so that some of us had a little time to hide or get away; everyone had to fend for herself because there was no one to protect us. Then they entered our room. There was general bedlam, girls shrieking, jumping from bed to bed, soldiers laughing, grabbing them, bunk platforms crashing. I hid at the end of the top-level bunk, curled up into the smallest bundle, covering myself with a blanket, shaking, and praying. I didn't know where Anyu was. When the solders left, the noise quieted down. I crawled down and saw the women in the middle of the room, their clothes disheveled, trembling, holding on to each other, sobbing. No one talked; not one word was uttered. The day that started with so much promise, so much joy, ended in bitter disappointment and consummate terror. Our dreams were shattered—the nightmare came without sleep.

"And it was morning and it was evening…" the first day of our liberation. We could not console each other. We resembled a group of beaten animals, licking our wounds. We knew we had to get out of the camp, as soon as possible.

ON THE WAY HOME, May–June, 1945

The morning after the "Liberation," 15 of us formed a group that stayed together until we got back to Hungary: Anyu, who was the oldest, my Aunt Lilli, and I, the youngest, as well as some distant relatives from Miskolc and Edeleny. We walked out of the camp, which was now unlocked, and went to town to find a place to stay. We needed to organize and manage to take care of ourselves until we found a way to leave and get back to our home in Hungary.

Although there were many Germans who did not leave town, the most affluent ones and those most clearly affiliated with the Nazi regime had escaped. In the distance we saw large groups of German people walking, women with children, old and young, leaving the city, perhaps anticipating punishment for their deeds, or perhaps just fearing the unknown future. I looked at them with pity, remembering our own march when leaving our homes, and I told my mother that I felt sorry for them. My mother snickered, reminding me that no one had shed a tear when we were driven out, and she scolded me for my "weakness."

We broke into one of the abandoned houses, a large mansion, with many rooms, but we all stayed together in the entry hall, which was as large as a living room. We felt safer being near the door. We sat down on the floor and

107

had a conference. Our first concern was to get some food; we searched the house
but found nothing. Then we divided the group—some were to stay in the house,
and four of us were to go out and to find something to eat. By now hunger had
again overtaken our consciousness. We did not dare go back to the camp where
we might have found something in the kitchen, but also would have met our
"liberators," the soldiers. In spite of our fear of the Russian soldiers in the city
itself, we felt it would be less dangerous to encounter them on the streets in the
center of the city than in a confined area, such as the camp.

The town was in chaos, and we just followed the crowd. Survivors
and perhaps others were looting homes and businesses. We passed by beautiful
homes and gardens. I looked longingly inside the gates, fell behind the others,
and stopped at one mansion with the name on the door: FARBEN. Could this be
the house that belonged to the owner of the factory for which we were forced to
work? Was this a coincidence? I felt the blood rushing into my face, and my heart
was beating like a drum. I waited and looked around; there was no sign of anyone
living there. I tried the door. It was open, and I entered. I saw a magnificent room,
with high heavily draped windows, lush carpeting underfoot, massive ornate
furniture, and beautiful paintings on the walls. And there, near the window, was
a polished black baby grand piano, beckoning me to try its shiny black and white
keys.

I always wanted to learn to play, but we could not afford to buy a piano,
or pay for lessons, so I only dreamed about it. But instead of putting my fingers
gently on the keys, a terrible, uncontrollable, destructive urge came over me. I
found a gold-handled cane in one corner, went to the piano, opened the top and
pulled the handle of the cane over the strings breaking them amidst their wailing
sounds. Then I started to beat everything that was in front of my eyes: I tore
into the petitpoint upholstered chairs, the silk brocade sofas. I smashed the glass

vitrines that held Meissen porcelains, like the ones we used to have in our home.
I saw the paintings of old masters on the walls through tears in my eyes, and I
stabbed them with the point of the cane. In my fury I had attacked the objects
of beauty I loved because I could only feel rage over the Nazis' utter betrayal of
things I believed in, of culture, art, civilization.

Then I was spent. I sat on the floor and sobbed until I was completely
depleted. After a while I got up and searched for something, I wasn't sure what. I
did not want to take any treasures as many had done on that first day of revenge.
I opened the cabinets, pulled out drawers, and I found what I was looking for—a
white tablecloth, an apron, and a small silver cup, with the initials EF engraved.
Did this cup belong to the owner, Farben, or, I fantasized, could it be that it was
the *Kiddush* cup of my grandfather, whose initials were EF? I held the three
objects, closed my eyes, and I saw my family's white tablecloth on the Shabbat
table, my grandmother wearing the apron, my grandfather, the silver cup in his
hand, saying the blessing over the wine. I knew I had to have these objects,
not because of their value, but because I was looking for something that would
connect me to my home, to my family, to our way of life. I walked out of the
mansion without searching for food, and with the precious bundle under my arm,
I returned to the house we occupied.

Anyu and the others surrounded me:

"Where were you? And where is the food? What is in this bundle?" they
questioned me anxiously.

"I can't explain it all now. Something happened to me that I do not
understand. I'll tell you later. But now, please guard this bundle, because there
are priceless treasures inside it. Now I have to run to catch up with the others."

I found most of the food stores already broken into; people were carrying
stuff in sacks and boxes. As I walked down the street, I met the old German

Arbeitsfuhrer from the factory who once gave me an apple. He was a tall, gaunt-looking man with a bird-like balding head. I wanted to thank him for his kindness in the factory, but he turned away from me in anger and said: "So, this is what I deserve? I never want to see another Jew again." Perhaps his home was also ransacked, I didn't know. I felt shame and regret. I wished I could have protected him, that I could have put a sign in his window, saying: "Here lives a decent German," the way Joshua's men in the biblical story had protected the harlot who hung a scarlet rope from her window. Although I didn't have anything in my hands, I felt embarrassed—I wanted to apologize to him. I wondered what he expected from me, whether he expected protection from the looters because he had once given me an apple. Or was he just like the others, soulless in his obedience to the Nazi rules, and had softened his heart only once when he gave me the apple? I couldn't contemplate too long, as he turned the corner and disappeared.

By the time we reached the bakery, it was almost emptied out, but we were able to get the last loaf of bread. Our next stop was the butcher shop where people were emptying the racks and cases, pushing and shoving each other. I squeezed in between two men, and on my tiptoes I grabbed a half a pig off the hook, threw it over my shoulder, and carried it triumphantly back to the group. There were no more stores to loot—everything was empty. I arrived at the house and stopped at the door as my mother looked at me in shock. Just then I feared that while the pig might save us from starving, my mother, an Orthodox Jew who had owned a kosher restaurant back home, might not accept it and would not let us eat it. But to my surprise she took the pig from my hands, cut it into pieces, found a big pot in the kitchen, and started boiling it. The unfamiliar smell made us nauseous but my mother practically commanded us:

"The 15 of us cannot possibly survive on one loaf of bread, and it looks like the Russians will not feed us. We have no choice—we must eat. Now that we are free, we must get home and find our families, and God will forgive us."

She shouldered all the responsibility, and we felt relieved. And with that she ceremoniously took the first piece, closed her eyes, and took a bite.

"What blessing do we say for pork?" I asked, innocently. We all ate boiled pork that night, and we all got sick, throwing up every bit of the food, not to our surprise. Then we barricaded the door with heavy furniture and finally fell asleep on the marble floor, near the entrance.

The old familiar hunger became a grave problem. We could no longer steal because the Russian soldiers were patrolling the streets, and they shot people on the spot, indiscriminately. We heard that some people had gone to the Russian military headquarters and had asked for some food and that they were taken away, possibly put into a labor camp. My cousin Elza decided that she and my mother would venture out of the house and look for work. After a day's search, they found a farmer who would let them work for food, and they started the following day. We had no choice; the liberated slaves were forced to work for the defeated Germans so that we could eat. We felt ourselves lucky because they saved us from starvation. Anyu and Elza returned every evening, exhausted, with bags of potatoes, bread, and other food.

Now that we had solved the problem of hunger, we could turn our attention to our goal of finding our way home. The group entrusted my cousin Fradi and me to investigate the possibilities that existed. We were told that in order to leave town, we needed to get permission from the German authorities whose offices were to be found in the next community, Peterswaldau.

We set out on foot and arrived just in time before the offices closed. We were led into a room, and the man in charge, sitting behind a big desk puffing his pipe, questioned us: "Where do you want to go? Where is your home? How will you get there?"

After we answered his questions as best as we could, he filled out some papers on the stationery of the mayor of the town and put his stamp on them. We took the papers with trembling hands. It was a "To Whom It May Concern" type of letter. On it he had written that we were liberated from concentration camps and wished to return to our home in Hungary; he requested that we be given assistance in reaching our destination. We were overjoyed and took our long walk back to Langenbielau. Of course, this letter alone would not guarantee that we could get permission from the Soviet authorities to leave town, nor did we have any idea how to travel. We heard that most of the railroads were bombed, but we hoped that some trains were still running.

Soon our plans fell into place. We found out that the Soviets would not give us permission to leave; they wanted the former slaves to continue to work for them. We knew that we had to find some other way to get out of town. By now my mother had befriended the German farmer, and he agreed to take us to the railroad station in his horse-drawn wagon, hiding us under the straw. Ironically, it was the German, the former enemy, who came to our aid. The next morning at dawn he appeared at our mansion; we all scrambled into his wagon, and he covered us with straw. We barely dared to breathe. He snapped his whip over the horses as they trudged slowly toward the railroad station. He let us off at the depot and left hurriedly.

The station was deserted, but after a couple of hours we heard the whistle blowing and indeed a freight train stopped and picked up some lumber. We sneaked into the cars and the train pulled away. Even though we had the letter from the mayor's office, we were not sure that the conductor would find it sufficient and allow us to stay on the train. Fortunately he did, and he made no fuss about us remaining in the cars. We were so deliriously happy until, a few hours later, the train stopped and would go no farther. We left the cars and went looking for water when suddenly the train started to move again. Frantically, we climbed aboard, but I noticed that Anyu and Frimet were left behind. The train was going slowly; I saw them running alongside and yelled back to the others who were in the cars behind ours: "Please, please, pull them up!" Some of the girls succeeded in grabbing their arms and dragged them up before the train gained speed. "I almost lost you again," I said with a shaky voice and held tight to her arm.

After a few hours of traveling, the engine suddenly came to a screeching halt, and the conductor made us get off. The train went back to where we started. We were tired and weary, not knowing where we would spend the night or how we would go on. We entered the station. It was deserted, not a soul around. We had no choice but to stay there overnight or until another train might come by. Again, we were frightened that some Soviet soldiers might come by, so we barricaded the door with benches and tried to sleep. Sure enough, drunken singing woke us in the middle of the night. They kept banging on the door, but eventually they gave up and left.

The next morning there was still no train in sight. Later in the day some of us decided to walk into the city. As usual, we were looking for food. We started walking toward the town but, just like the station, it was deserted. The houses and buildings were in ruins, bombed out, staircases leading to nowhere, a lonely chimney reaching toward the sky. The road was dusty, the pavement covered with rubble. There were no other people around, no movement, just us in an eerie silence. The Germans must have left either in the midst of bombing, or had escaped in a hurry from the occupying army.

We kept walking. The sun was quickly moving toward the horizon; we had to hurry if we were to find something before it got dark. As we were approaching the town square, we saw two people sitting on a bench. From a distance we couldn't tell who they were, and we were reluctant to get closer to them. I took a few more steps and was able to see an old man and an old woman. They were facing each other, the woman bending her head, while the man seemed to hold her head in his hands. I couldn't figure out what they were doing, but suddenly I felt as if I were an intruder, as if I had no right to be there, and I quickly withdrew behind a tree. After a few minutes I peeked out from behind the tree and saw it: the old lady's long, gray hair covered her face, she was bending down as if she were also hiding in her shame. The man, withered and bespectacled, was parting the strands of her hair, gently and patiently, cracking lice between his fingernails. There were no words between them and except for his fingers, they were motionless, almost frozen. I shivered and touched my own short hair. I waited behind the tree until the flaming red sun sank below the skeletons of the crumbling buildings. I just stood there, my eyes glued on the ancient couple, my body melted into the tree, watching as the sun's rays lit up and transformed her gray hair into a golden halo.

We got back to the station just in time to see a train approaching, and, to our great relief, it slowed down and stopped. As if responding to a command, we all climbed aboard and realized that this was not a freight car but a passenger train. Could this be the beginning of a normal life, traveling like human beings? It was hard to believe! We took seats; I sat next to my mother, near the window. I saw my image in the window—a thin small face with short hair. Suddenly I remembered how long my hair used to be when I was in Junior High School, the last school that I had attended. Two long braids tightly pulled away from my face to match my equally severe-looking school uniform. But when the Hungarian

Nazis closed our school, I cut my braids and threw them in the river under our window. From then on I wore my hair loose, unbound, and I used to throw my head back with a defiant shake the way I had seen it done by my movie idol, Karadi Katalin. I remembered how I thought at that time that from then on, I would always be free and unfettered.

"Cover your head," my mother admonished me and brought me back to reality. "If the Russian soldiers see you, they may take you away." I wished I had my lavender kerchief but it was just a rag that I pulled over my head, then I leaned against my mother and dozed off.

I was awakened by loud banging on the cabin door and the now-familiar drunken yelling of the soldiers, *barishna, barishna*. The doors were pushed open and in walked three uniformed Soviet army men. We pulled back on our seats, trying to make ourselves invisible. It was night and there was only a dim light in the cabin. Some of the girls could speak Polish, and they tried to talk to the soldiers and explain to them who we were. Then one of them, a short young man, exclaimed in Yiddish: "Are you Jewish maidens, my sisters I lost long ago? Are you my people?" And he opened his arms and embraced the girl and then the next one and the next one and wept on their shoulders. Then he and his comrades reassured us that they would stay at the door and protect us from any intruders while we traveled on this train.

The next morning two other men got on the train; they were also ex-inmates, recently liberated by the Soviets. One of them approached me and said in Yiddish: "I want to give you some jewelry to make yourself pretty," and he showed me some rings and necklaces. He must have looted a jewelry store during those first days after liberation when everyone stole whatever they could and bought food with it. He obviously had no need for the jewelry otherwise. But when he saw us, girls in rags, all our feminine beauty gone, he must have felt a desire to make someone happy.

"Here, choose whatever you want or take it all!" I looked at him in disbelief, then turned to my mother, questioningly. "Could I accept it?" I was going to say, but before I could utter the words, Anyu shook her head vigorously, and I knew the answer:

"You don't accept a gift from a man, especially jewelry, because he might say the blessing that a groom utters at his wedding: 'With this ring, you are betrothed to me as my wife.' If he says that and you accept the gift, it is as if you married him," explained my mother. My father had taught me this since I was a little girl, but I never imagined that it would ever happen to me. I looked at the jewelry with a wistful heart, but I knew that I could not accept it. The young man couldn't understand why I refused his offer and moved on to others who eagerly took the gold.

After about two weeks of train rides, often going back to where we started, we finally arrived at the Western border of Hungary. The city of Bratislava was known to us as Pressburg, or in Hungarian, Pozsony. It was night when our train stopped. There were thousands of people at the station, pushing, shoving, trying to get on the train. Soldiers of all nationalities jammed the platform and pushed themselves on the steps and into the cabins. Suddenly I was lifted and thrown out the window by a Hungarian soldier, and the rest of us followed. The Rumanian soldiers thought this was a fun game, and they picked us up and threw us back into the cabin, which was pitch dark, and we landed on top of the soldiers.

I remembered that being too close to soldiers, of any nationality, was not a healthy thing, since seeing girls, even former prisoners like us, made the soldiers wild and uncontrolled. I climbed up into the luggage rack, pulled Anyu up, and there we lay quietly, until the rhythmic movement of the train lulled me to sleep. When the early rays of the sun woke me, I saw Lilli peacefully sleeping in the arms of a handsome Hungarian soldier. Nobody raped any one of us on that train, and we were grateful for our good fortune. As the train slowly chugged along toward the east, we yelled out the names of the towns and cities as we remembered them from our geography lessons. My heart was beating almost as loudly as the wheels of the train when we finally arrived in Budapest.

IS THIS OUR HOME? — June 1945

Budapest, the capital of Hungary, was in rubble. We walked around bombed-out buildings, looking for streets that were no longer there. Lilli and I left Anyu and the others at the railroad station. We headed toward that part of the city where Lilli used to live with my grandparents before they had moved back to Edeleny to avoid the bombings. We knew we would not find anyone there, yet Lilli still wanted to see the place where she had spent a few happy years. We climbed up the stairs, knocked on the door. Strangers came to the door; and we asked if we could go in and just see the rooms. We entered and stood there, waiting for some miracle, for someone dear to us to appear. But the walls offered no solace, and we left.

My Aunt Ilonka and her family used to live in the Jewish section of the city, which later became the ghetto, and where most of the synagogues, butcher shops, and Jewish Community offices were located. We passed by them, without looking, because we wanted to find my aunt as soon as we could. We finally arrived at Paulai Edde Utca 20, an apartment house of several stories with a rectangular courtyard and balconies on four sides. I raced up the stairs with Lilli, found the door and knocked timidly—no answer.

"They must be here," I said to Lilli. "Didn't they tell us that most of the Jews of Budapest were able to escape deportation?" I said and decided to knock harder. After a few minutes we heard the shuffling of slippers and a thin voice came from inside, "Who is it?" I looked at Lilli questioningly, and finally the door opened a crack. An old neighbor of my Aunt Ilonka, the one who had lived on the floor above them, saw us and cried out in surprise:

"Oh, my God, you came back." She embraced us warmly. I was glad to see her but didn't dare ask her about my aunt. I could not face learning about the fate of those who were left in Budapest, but she volunteered:

"Your aunt and her children are alive. They moved to Miskolc after the liberation, where your uncle Hermus has a home, and they all live together. Ilonka's husband, Mishi, was taken away by the Nazis and killed. Your other aunt, Edith, also moved there with her baby, Noemi, because her husband, Bumi, was shot and thrown into the Danube. My husband was also taken away and now I am all alone."

She cried silently. This was our first encounter with the reality of our losses. My lips stuck together. I reached out to her, my arms held on to her body, tears wetting my face. There was nothing to say. We hurried back to the station, got on the next train, and started on the last leg of our journey, toward our home, Miskolc.

My racing thoughts kept pace with the rhythmic motion of the locomotive. I wanted to be there already, back home, back where everything was. Then fear grabbed my stomach, twisting and turning. I wanted to avoid getting there, and I wanted to hide under the bed, the way I used to do when I was a child and something frightened me. What if there was nobody there, I thought, what if there was no house, what if nobody wants me there? I was aching to share my anxiety with Anyu, but I held back. Why make her more nervous, I said to myself—better if we don't talk.

It was late afternoon when the train stopped. The same sun that so often had given me warmth and reassurance now hung on the horizon, impersonally. From the window I saw people standing in groups on the platform, bunched together, as if waiting for some judgment. I jumped off the last step and started running toward them when I saw my long-lost brother, Yitzhak, running toward us. He reached for my mother and held her for a long time before he would embrace me.

"You are here, you are really here, you came back!" he cried, and he kept touching us to make sure we were real. Then others approached us, friends of the family, happy to see us, the big question in their eyes: have you seen my mother, my sister, my wife? We told them what we knew, often revealing something that they already knew.

"How did you know we were coming?" I asked my brother.

"We didn't know. But we have been coming to the railroad station every day, since we ourselves came back. We are here every day, making sure that when someone arrives, there would be somebody waiting for him."

My Uncle Hermus lived in a nice house, and every day the walls stretched as more of us moved in: five women, two men, and four children. Then some cousins needed a place to stay, and we made room for them also. One day, my friend Gabi asked if she could stay with us. She was alone, her parents were killed, and she didn't know what had happened to her brothers. "I can't bear coming home with no one there to open the door; the house is empty. Please can I stay with your family for a while?"

Our former maid, Mari, came to see us. She brought a pillow case, saying that she would sew me a blouse from it. It was pink and beautiful. A few days later she brought me a comforter lining, pinkish red, which used to encase the feathers, which became my skirt.

"It is a perfect match," I exclaimed happily. "I found a perfect match."

We were told to go to the Jewish Community offices where they were distributing food provided by the Joint Distribution Committee, an American philanthropic agency that helped the Jews overseas. We received a box of goodies; we opened the canned tuna hesitatingly since we had never eaten it before, danced with joy when we received apples and oranges, but looked with suspicion at the golden bananas, asking if we needed to cook them. There were other goodies in our packages—priceless needles and thread, combs, soaps, and pencils to write with.

The janitor of the building and his family had occupied our apartment where we had lived before we were deported. They said they were happy that we came back, but I wasn't sure. Eventually they moved out and found another place to live, taking with them part of our furniture. We had no income so my mother decided that she would re-open the restaurant to earn a few dollars. Of course we had no equipment, but we got some from the officers of the Jewish Community who were eager to have a kosher kitchen for people who returned and had no homes. My brother Yitzhak found *gescheften*, work, as it was called, buying and selling stuff that he could get on the black market. Inflation was one hundred percent; we needed to buy supplies the same evening we received whatever money he earned, because by morning we couldn't get anything for it.

One day a friend of my father came by and said, "On the 7th of the Hebrew month of *Adar*, you should light a *yahrzeit* candle because that's when your father was shot and killed. I was with him on that bitter winter day in February as we marched west of the Hungarian border, near Felixdorf, in Austria. Your father was very weak because he had refused to eat the non-kosher soup that was the only food we were given. He had valiantly held on to his beliefs till his last breath and recited the *Shema* before he was shot, at age 48. He wanted you to remember that."

Anyu sat silently with us in the same room. She and my brother had already learned about my father's death from others, but they needed this confirmation and wanted me to hear it. I sat there in a daze, looking at Anyu, questioning whether what the man told us was indeed true. She nodded her head sadly, but no words of comfort came from her lips, no reassuring touch, just a vacant stare in the air. I could not stand the tension—even though we, all three of us, suffered the loss, we could not comfort each other. Both Anyu and Yitzhak tried to stay calm and controlled. They feared expressing grief, as if had they allowed themselves to show the pain, they would not be able to stop it, and it would overwhelm them. I wished I could break through this silent acknowledgement of my father's death, but I also lacked courage to open up, and I just stayed within myself. Instead, I got up, left the house, and walked the streets till dark.

It was a few weeks later when I went to visit our former maid, Mari, who now worked for a doctor. I talked to her about my father and how I was waiting for the return of my younger brother, Moshu. She took my hand in hers and said that my brother would not return because he had died at the end of April, one week before he would have been liberated. I let out a scream:

"It's not true, it's not true! I just heard from two people who were with him in the forced labor camp what a wonderful friend he had been and how he tried to help others. He couldn't have died. They saw him in March. He was so well liked by the Hungarian officer for whom my brother became an errand boy. He was only 15 and worked like an adult. He even grew in the camp, became taller, a real *chevraman* (buddy), they said, so it can't be true!"

Mari looked at me with her intelligent brown eyes and said,

"All this was true. But they didn't tell you that the last few weeks Moshu became ill with typhus, and there was no medicine. The march went on, and they left him dying by the roadside."

She held my shaking body in her arms, wiping my tears, murmuring consoling words. When I left her, I knew that there was no one else to wait for. Yes, my grandparents, aunts, uncles, little cousins, all had been murdered. And now I knew that my father and my brother would never return. My mother had known about this, but could not bring herself to tell me. We finally cried together that evening.

One day I went by a neighbor's house and looked in the window and saw our own dining room furniture neatly arranged, as if it belonged there.

"But it is ours!" I tried to convince Anyu to claim it back, saying, "They had no right to take what belongs to us. I am sure if you tell them, they will give it back to you. Please, try."

I wanted that furniture because I wanted my old life back. I wanted order, and I wanted to trust again in the future. Apu always reminded us not to step on the furniture, not to ruin it because it would have to be nice when suitors came to the house. Now my father was gone, but I wanted the furniture. My mother agreed, and one day, she knocked on the neighbor's door and asked for the furniture.

"Why? Why would I give you back the furniture when it no longer belongs to you? It is mine. After all, you left the country and now you have no right to take it back. Why did you come back, anyway?" and with that he slammed the door in her face.

Frightening events started to take place again in our beloved city.

Two Jews were caught by an angry mob when they were accused of negotiating a deal on the black market. They tied them to a wagon by a rope and dragged them through the streets, killing them amidst the cheers of many onlookers. "Hitler did not finish his job. More of them came back than left," they yelled. The Jews stayed behind their locked doors and fear swept through the "remnants" again. Neither the occupying soldiers nor the Hungarian police tried to rescue the unfortunate men.

The Soviet army that had liberated Hungary stayed on. There were soldiers everywhere, and they appropriated anything they needed without paying for it. Sometimes they would come into our restaurant and demand food and drink, and Anyu hastened to satisfy them lest they become more belligerent or even threaten to take my brother away. I usually hid in the kitchen, but one day one of them noticed me and commanded my mother to bring me out. "Pretty girl, come with me. I'll give you a watch," and he showed me his arm which already had six watches on it. I did not answer but rushed into our bedroom where we had hidden a bottle of vodka that my brother had gotten for just such an occasion, and brought it to the table. The soldier's face lit up and he poured himself a glass of the drink, urging me to join him. After he gulped down the second glass, he started singing, then drinking again. Suddenly there was a loud noise from the street and it gave me the chance to get up and run outside, and I stayed behind the gate of the next building. A few minutes later I watched him stagger out the door and walk away. That evening I was sure that this could never be my home again.

"WHY DID I SURVIVE?" —
Miskolc, 1945, to Budapest, 1947

In the weeks and months following our return, I often felt confused and disoriented. Every day we learned about the fate of those who did not return. We heard about the miraculous escape from mass deportation of most of the Jews of Budapest. We listened to the stories of their survival in the Ghetto, hiding as non-Jews, and in the "protected houses" that were established by Swedish and Swiss diplomats who issued *Schutzpasse*, or protective passes. Nothing made sense any more. Why was I saved? Why me?

I kept asking myself these questions but I found no answers. I remembered my saintly father, who prayed every day and who was so honest that he would not charge his customers more than what we absolutely needed for our modest survival. Why was he murdered? Or my innocent younger brother, Moshu, who would not kill a fly. Why did he perish? I wanted so much to share my thoughts and feelings with my mother, or with any other adult, but I didn't dare. I did not want to upset her or anyone, so I struggled with them alone. I was looking for something that would explain it all, to help me find some direction in my life. I was searching for something I could dedicate my life to—it almost did not matter what—just something I could be part of, to fill the gaping void.

Then I heard about a group that usually gathered at the synagogue, and I was eager to meet them. Indeed, I found a group of boys and girls, all of whom had lost their families and were searching, like me, for some comfort, for some meaning in their lives. There was a young man there who spoke eloquently about *Eretz Yisrael*, or Palestine, and urged us all to go and live there, to build the country, because Hungary could no longer be our home. He then invited us to join the religious Zionist youth organization, called *"Bnei-Akiba,"* and become pioneers of the land. He informed us also that the organization had a summer camp, near Miskolc, and invited us to participate.

I was spellbound by the young man's ideas—I would have followed him anywhere. I felt he showed me that I could do something with my life, that I mattered. I was also enthusiastic about his proposal about the summer camp, but my mother wasn't sure. She was waiting to hear from her brothers in Mexico who by now must have found out that we were alive. She was hesitant about allowing me to go to camp because, she said, it would not be proper for boys and girls to be together. But I think the real reason was that she didn't want me out of her sight. Eventually, with the help of my brother, Yitzhak, I convinced Anyu to let me go, and I embarked on the journey that gave direction to my life. I was lucky to have found a group that espoused ideas so close to my tradition and family values. I was so hungry and desperate to belong somewhere that had I gotten into a group that advocated less salutary ideas, I might have gone with them as well, simply to avoid the terrible emptiness.

Moshava was the name of the summer camp. It was situated in the little town of Vadna, in a hilly, forested area with green meadows and a little brook that made me feel as if I were looking out at the little *Szinva* creek that ran under the windows of our home. We spent our days exercising and hiking. We studied history, Zionism, and often got into deep intellectual discussions. In the evenings we sat around the campfire, each of us recalling our stories, our families. One older boy, who was always very serious, took me for a walk one evening and told me that we should not talk to people outside the camp about what happened to us. He said that those who had not gone through what we had would not believe us. He also believed that people would not want to hear these stories, or worse, that they would accuse us of lying. This had happened to him. But here in the camp we were with friends; they would understand. His words stuck in my mind for a long time, and I was always conscious of not revealing too much about our past suffering to "outsiders."

One night the leader of the group, who was just a few years older than we were, asked us to think about why we survived, why we were saved when so many others perished, and asked us to share our thoughts. I heard one after the other saying something about not knowing, not understanding, but that we must have a special task, a certain divinely-ordered assignment to carry out if we were spared. I heard the words, I watched their faces lit up by the dancing flames of the campfire, and I wanted to say, yes, we do have something important to do; otherwise we don't deserve to live either. But when it was my turn to say something, the words stuck in my throat, tears blinded my eyes, and it took a few minutes until I blurted out:

"I still have my mother. I am more fortunate than you. I feel more guilty than you, and I don't know why I deserve to be alive." I felt ashamed; I just wanted to cry and was grateful that they let me do that.

A young man about my brother's age approached me the following night. His name was Avigdor, he was from the western part of Hungary, and he survived the war together with one sister. He had a beautiful, soft voice, and he taught the

129

group Hebrew songs in the evenings around the campfire. I was eager to learn these songs, and when he talked to me that evening, I felt privileged and excited. He was a very handsome boy with dark eyes and a warm smile, and most of the girls were dying to get his attention.

"I like you," he said simply. "I would like you to be my friend, my *bachura* (girlfriend). I need someone like you who can say what she feels because I have so many confusing feelings myself, and I have no one who will listen to me."

Why me, I thought, why did he choose me, when there were other, even smarter or prettier girls here? What did he mean when he said he liked me? How could we be friends? He lived far away, and besides, my mother would never allow me to have a boyfriend. I was too young, she would say. I didn't even know what he meant by "friend." Did he mean girlfriend, and if he did, what would that mean? Thoughts raced through my mind, and I had no answer for him. He sat next to me, we looked at the sky with its countless flickering stars, and I let him put his arm around me.

After the *Moshava* I became active in the movement. We had endless discussions about what we could do to be worthy of our survival. We sang Hebrew songs, danced Israeli dances, and decided to study the language of our future country seriously. I had already started to take lessons in the Hebrew language before the deportation, but now I became more dedicated to studying it. When an invitation came from Budapest to attend a seminar for youth leaders, I was happy to hop on the train and become one of the participants. This was when I learned about the history of the *Aliyot*, or the waves of immigration to Palestine, legal and illegal; about the development of the *Kibbutz* movement; about the "ideal Jew" who would work for the land and at the same time study and live by the precepts of the Torah. I finally found what I was looking for—something that would give purpose to my life. One of the instructors was Jakubovics Emil, or Menahem Uziel, my future husband.

Meanwhile my cousin Ancsi [or Andy as he is called now], the only surviving member of his family, came to live with us. He was a year younger than I—my little brother's age—and I dragged him with me to the meetings. I wanted him to become a Zionist and fulfill the dream of settling in Israel. He had no parents who would object, and after we made a promise to each other that we would always remain "brother and sister," we even pricked our fingers and let our blood mingle, signifying our eternal bond. Soon he joined the group that left with the illegal *Aliyah,* to emigrate to Palestine. Unfortunately, his ship was intercepted by the British who at that time would not allow any ship to land in Palestine, and Andy ended up on the island of Cyprus, together with hundreds of other survivors who were denied entry to Palestine.

Later, when the State of Israel was proclaimed and the Arab nations attacked the new state, my cousin Andy found himself in the Israeli army, the *Haganah.*" When his comrades fell one after another, Andy could no longer handle these new losses. He was hospitalized with a complete nervous breakdown. I could not forgive myself for having influenced him to go there. After he recovered, relatives in America helped him come to the States and get an education.

In the summer of 1946, I again joined the group to go to summer camp, which was now near Lake Balaton, in the western part of Hungary. This time I was already a junior counselor, with ten to twelve young orphaned girls in my charge. The program of the camp included training for an illegal landing in Palestine. We learned to fight and defend ourselves with clubs, to climb ropes that stretched over deep ditches and water, simulating real landings.

All this time my mother and the rest of the family were hoping to go to Mexico where three uncles, who had immigrated to Mexico before the outbreak of the war, were living. They tried very hard to get us out of Hungary, which was now Communist controlled with closed borders, to join them in Mexico. Meanwhile my brother Yitzhak was intensely involved in the *B'richa*, an organization dedicated to smuggling people out of the countries that were now under Communist rule and to facilitating their flight to Palestine. The Soviets, who then occupied Hungary, often intercepted their escapes and arrested them. We stayed up nights worrying when my brother did not return in time from one of the border-crossing trips.

Yitzhak later told us that during one of these escapades, a Soviet officer demanded that he hand over the identification papers of the Jews whom my brother tried to get through the border. While the officer turned away, my brother swallowed some of the papers, and thus the names of the Jews were not revealed. But he could only extricate himself after he bribed the officers with a large amount of money. The Jews of Palestine and America had sent this money to the *B'richa*.

My mother decided to move up to Budapest after the tragedy of the two murdered Jews, and now I was able to continue my work with orphaned children. I also enrolled in the Teacher's Institute of the Jewish Theological Seminary and continued my studies in Hebrew and other subjects. I was no longer interested in Avigdor, because he wanted too much of my attention. One day he shaved his head because I would not stroke it enough. He was too serious about our relationship. He wanted a commitment, but I was not ready for it—I was happier having several boys running after me. Anyu also felt safer that way, but she would still stand at the window every time I went out until I returned home at night.

My uncles in Mexico kept urging us to learn a trade that would help us earn a living when we got to Mexico. I complied and went to a Communist-controlled union shop to learn to make leather purses. I was careless about my interaction with others, and the plant manager accused me of being a counter-revolutionary and warned me that I would be arrested if I didn't stop. I had no idea what I was doing wrong, but I thought it would be better if I quit the place, and I sent a message that I was ill and could not continue. The Communist manager fortunately accepted my excuse for not reporting to work. Because of his accusations, I could have been arrested for expressing ideas that sounded anti-government to him. Instead, to satisfy my uncles, I started to take Spanish classes though I did not want to go to Mexico. My whole being ached to go to Palestine, to become a *chalutza* (pioneer), but my mother would not agree.

Jakubovics Emil, Menachem, in Hebrew (Uzi, his nickname), was one of the top leaders of the youth movement. He was a young man who was originally from Csap, the Northeastern part of the country (originally Czechoslovakia), and who attended the University of Budapest, studying for his Ph.D. He was one of five young men who led the B'nei Akiba in Hungary. During the war he worked in the underground, helping people escape from Hungary to Rumania and from there to Palestine. His parents, Benjamin and Rivkah Jakubovics, and his two younger siblings, Shalom and Miriam, were murdered in the gas chambers of Auschwitz, but his brother, Cvi and his sisters, Chana and Malka survived the camps. All three of them left Hungary after the war and emigrated to Palestine through Rumania.

Uzi and his friends comprised this group of five young leaders of the organization, established group homes for orphans, created schools and summer camps, academic and social programs for youth. Uzi was in charge of the overall organization of the movement and executed the carrying out the illegal *Aliyah* (emigration) from Hungary, through Austria, Rumania, and the Balkans, and later, through France. Because during the German occupation, he had created an escape route from the Nazis through Rumania and the Black Sea to Palestine, he was already experienced in rescue efforts.

In 1947 the summer camp again was at the Balaton, and the program continued with the training for illegal landings in Palestine and the establishment of new kibbutz settlements. Uzi was the director of the camp that summer, and I was eager to get his attention, but he usually ignored me. One night I got hold of a pocketknife, sneaked behind his pup tent, and cut the rope that attached the tent to a tree. The tent collapsed, and I ran to my tent before I could be discovered. The next morning at the flag raising, we all stood in attention while Uzi made a speech, admonishing "those" who hadn't yet learned to build, only to ruin, to dismantle. He did not point a finger at me, but everyone knew whom he meant. But the trick worked, I apologized, and he got to know me, and soon the songs around the campfire had already made us into a couple. When Anyu heard about this, she decided to pay an unexpected visit to the camp, which was several hours away by truck from Budapest. She was relieved when she saw that our relationship was quite innocent, and instead of making me leave the camp, *she* left the next day.

My family was feverishly preparing to leave the country, but the Mexican government refused to give visas to Jews. So instead of waiting any longer in Hungary, my uncles arranged visas for us to go to Cuba. We, the remainder of our family in Hungary, my Uncle Hermush, his new wife, Manyi, my mother, my brother Yitzhak, who from then on used his Hungarian name of Zoltan, and I were ready for our new life on the tropical island of Cuba. My Aunt Edith, who survived the war with her little girl Noemi in Budapest, had also remarried, but to our great sorrow she died in childbirth weeks before we were to leave. My Aunt

Ilonka, who also lost her husband in the war and had remained with her three little children, was also to leave Hungary with us. They, however, were able to get permission to enter Mexico because my Uncle Itzu in Mexico had adopted the children. So my aunt took Noemi with her, the orphaned child of her deceased sister, Edit, and Noemi became her fourth child.

Anyu found the many volumes of my father's *Talmud* in the basement under the coal where we had hidden them before the deportation. Together with our few personal belongings, we packed them in big boxes and shipped them directly to Mexico. Only then was it clear to me that I had no choice but to go with them to Cuba.

Meanwhile, everybody we knew was trying to get out of the country, and most of them went to Palestine. No matter how I begged my mother, how I tried to convince her that as Jews we could only go to our ancient homeland and not to some exotic, foreign country where we were unwelcome, it was to no avail. "The family has to stay together. Maybe later you can live there, but not now," she said. But I didn't give up and was still hoping that in the last minute she would relent.

Uzi, who was now almost 24, and I, 19 in May, became serious about one another. Although I had many boyfriends before, none of them possessed the qualities that drew me to Uzi. Besides being kind, intelligent, analytic, and "cool," what impressed me most was that he had the ability to negotiate between people who were in conflict and always find a peaceful solution to the problem. As he was a Zionist youth leader, I knew that he would go only to Eretz Yisrael. Since the summer of 1947, he had become a frequent guest in our home, and my mother saw that our relationship was very important to us. She was torn—she wanted her daughter to be happy, but she could not be apart from me. Neither could I leave her, nor would I give up my boyfriend. Finally Uzi and I came to an interim solution: I would travel with my family to Cuba, and after Anyu got settled there, I would join Uzi in Palestine. Uzi agreed to this but only if we were formally engaged before we left.

Saturday, November 29th, 1947, was a momentous day in our lives. In the morning Uzi and I walked to the University of Pazmany Peter, the Hungarian National University, where he officially received his Ph.D. On that day the United Nations voted on the establishment of a Jewish state, named Israel. And in the evening of that very same day, Uzi and I got engaged in my aunt's home. My mother broke a plate, as was the custom. I received a ring and a bracelet from my fiancé, purchased with money he had borrowed from his good friend, Pinchas Rosenbaum. I cried all the way home. The next day was Uzi's 24th birthday, and my mother cooked some special sausages to celebrate. Two days later, on Tuesday, December 2, 1947, our train left Budapest, toward Vienna, Switzerland and France. Uzi accompanied us as far as the Austrian border, and then we said goodbye, not knowing when or how we would ever see each other again.

JOURNEY TO THE FREE WORLD —
The Cuban Adventure, 1947–1949

We sighed with relief as we crossed the Hungarian-Austrian border. The train took us through the unimaginable beauty of the Austrian and Swiss Alps. This time I was sitting in a regular passenger car, surrounded by the remnants of my family, traveling to the New World. I left my home that was no longer my home, and now I looked forward with anxious anticipation to a future in a strange country, among strange people. I left my fiancé Uzi in the hope that sometime, sooner or later, we would be reunited.

In Paris we were received by some friends, the Reisman boys, who decided to play a trick on us. They convinced us that we had to take a bath in the municipal bathhouse as newcomers to the city. They had played this joke on all their friends who had arrived there, and who, like us, believed that we had to go through some purification process, or delousing, before we could be admitted to a civilized society. Fortunately my little cousins were too much of a hassle to our friends and thus they confessed that this was just a joke on gullible refugees and that it was not really required.

Paris was wonderful and exotic, and we enjoyed the city even with the meager food rations we could acquire. I marveled at the beautiful women, dressed so chic, at the dogs that sat on chairs in the cafes next to their loving owners who fed them croissants. To top it all, our friends insisted that we accept their invitation to see the *Follies Bergere*. We sat in this elegant theatre dressed in our best clothes and eagerly awaited the program. But soon after it started, I felt tense and uncomfortable. I became very upset watching those pretty girls, their breasts bared, dancing, and lifting their long legs to the wild enthusiasm of the spectators. The last time I saw naked bodies was when we were forced to undress in front of the German soldiers in Auschwitz. Then it wasn't pretty or joyous—it was shameful and dreaded. I couldn't understand why these girls were willing to show their naked bodies voluntarily, when no one forced them. After a few days we left the city of lights and boarded the train again, to go to the seaport city of Calais. We were eager to leave, to get closer to our destination.

The English Channel was stormy, and as the ship threw us back and forth, from one side to the other, we all got sick. We finally arrived in Dover, England, where we took another train to London. We stayed in a cold and unfriendly rooming house where we put Hungarian coins into the heater, instead of English tokens, money we did not have, to make it work. London did not enchant us. We did marvel at the big department stores. We managed to see the British Museum while we waited for the ship that would take us from England to the United States, and we were ready to leave when the day of departure came.

The Queen Mary left the port of Southampton on a sunny winter day in December 1947. We all felt like we were in a fairy tale, this beautiful ship, with all the conveniences we had never heard of, with smiling and polite people who were there to serve us and provide for all our needs. I looked out to the sea from our deck, a sea without a horizon, an ocean that would bring us to the Promised

Land. The ship pulled out of the harbor, and that's the last I remembered. The following five days I lost awareness of my surroundings. The stormy sea rocked our ship as if it were a toy, and I lay there, either in the cabin, or on the windy, rainy deck, wet and covered with salt from the sea water, sick to my stomach, refusing any food. I made a vow that I would never again cross the ocean on a ship.

After five days we recognized the Statue of Liberty, beckoning its welcome to us to America. People were waving from the shore, but I didn't know anyone among them. Then as we disembarked, a tall man approached us, asked our name, and said that he was here as a relative, a member of the Horowitz-Margareten family, and he would take us to our hotel. His face was expressionless, he was chewing gum, and he spoke an incomprehensible English. After we received our trunks, we piled into two taxis, and he delivered us to the Broadway-Central Hotel, on the Lower East Side of Manhattan.

Soon other relatives came to see us, among them Aunt Rebus, or Regina Margareten, who was the head of the clan and of the matza factory. She was already in her 80s, but she remembered us from Hungary where she used to come to visit us in Edeleny. She was my grandfather's partner in the coal mine, and she and some of her children made a yearly pilgrimage to their original homeland, often bringing gifts to the little ones. She was an imposing, regal woman, who was still very active in her business. She brought us special Hungarian coffeecake that she had baked herself, and invited us to the upcoming Horowitz-Margareten family Chanukah celebration.

The Kramer family, also cousins of Anyu, helped us orient ourselves in this big city. On Friday afternoon, Florence, who was only 15, brought us food for our Shabbat dinner. Afterwards, she could not get home by bus because of a terrific snowstorm, and she had to walk on foot the entire way. I was impressed that she could do that by herself, but then I remembered the terrific snowstorms I had dragged myself and my mother through.

The following week they took us to the market, where we found all kinds of food we had only dreamed of until now—fruits and vegetables in the middle of winter, breads and cheeses of all kinds, sour cream the likes of which I had never eaten. We went to the market every day, and I ate bread with sour cream every day in our hotel room. One day my cousin Florence took us to Radio City Music Hall, and the lights and the music mesmerized me. We walked the streets of New York that had been decorated for Christmas. We stared at the windows of the stores, full of all kinds of beautiful clothes, shoes, toys, and furniture, and they took my breath away. We stopped at a newsstand and I looked at the multitude of newspapers and magazines, and I became dizzy. All this was there to read, and it was available for just a few pennies. And suddenly I became overwhelmed by such abundance; I felt as if I was again in the garbage dump, in one of the camps, where to my joy I found treasured food scraps when a new load of garbage was dumped on me and I almost suffocated. So much, too many good things, and I didn't know how to cope with it. Perhaps I felt unworthy to have all this richness, or didn't believe that such abundance could be had without negative consequences.

And it continued. My cousin Florence gave me a pretty dress to wear for the family party, which was held in a hotel, with music and fancy decorations and food and drinks and smiling faces. They welcomed us warmly and wished us good luck on our journey to Cuba. Nobody had asked us anything about the lives we left behind, about the years of deprivation and suffering. Nobody asked about our losses, the missing family. Everybody was happy, celebrating. I felt strange, out of place—I felt I did not belong there. Then someone asked me if I would sing a few Hebrew songs in honor of the vote in the United Nations for the establishment of Israel. I stood up on the podium and I sang, at first tentatively, then with more confidence, songs honoring the strength and hope of the Jewish people and the Jewish homeland. I got a standing ovation; though I am certain the applause was for my enthusiasm and for my willingness to stand up there, rather than for my musical ability.

The next day we said goodbye to my Aunt Ilonka and my four little cousins who left for Mexico. The rest of us, on a snowy winter morning, January 7th, 1948, boarded the plane in New York for the last leg of our trip, to the island of Cuba, the only country close to Mexico that would, for ample compensation by my uncles, issue visas to us. I had never flown on a plane before, so it was scary and exciting. A man named Rosenberg, who had arranged our visas, waited for us and took us to a hotel in downtown Havana.

In the hotel the air was hot and humid. The doors and windows of the room remained wide open as we tried to fall asleep in our new environment. The sound of strange music, and the beating of the drums coming from a club without walls across the street never stopped throughout the night. Eventually I gave up trying to sleep, and watched the people on the narrow streets from the balcony—the men, mostly dark skinned, dressed in white suits, and the women with Creole faces, in ruffled dresses, dancing, skipping to the beat of the strange African music. The flying tropical *cucarachas* had equal access to our hotel room and added to the spell of that first mystifying night in Havana.

The next day we were deposited in an apartment in the residential section of Havana, called Vedado, on a beautiful, palm-lined street, with a view of the blue-green Caribbean Sea. I shared a room with my mother and brother, but my aunt and uncle wanted their own place, and rented an apartment. We moved in with another refugee family, Yiddish-speaking Polish Jews who rented us a room and allowed us to use the kitchen. My mother and I shared a bed, and my

141

brother had his own bed in the same room. There were other refugees there as well. Although everyone in the apartment was from Europe and went through the Holocaust, we had little in common with the rest of the residents.

The woman who rented us the room, Mrs. Rosenkranz, collected everything from rags to papers, pots, clothes and shoes, and stored them in one room, especially set aside for that purpose. The place was full almost to the ceiling, *cucarachas* eating the soiled clothes, most of the items old or damaged. I asked her one day why she collected all those things, and she answered: "*Alles kenn men nutzen*," in Yiddish, meaning everything can be used, we may need it one day. She had lost everything during the war, and now she wanted to be sure that she would never be without whatever she needed. I understood it, did not question her again, and named the room *Nutzerei:* the place where things are kept that will be used some day.

My uncles in Mexico sent us the money for our room and for food, but we wanted to find a way to earn something ourselves, even though, as visitors to Cuba, we were not allowed to work. My brother found work on a chicken farm, and he brought eggs to the city for my mother to sell. She walked around the streets with a big basket on her arm, knocking on doors, making a few dollars every week. Then when my brother got tired of the chickens, he and I took costume jewelry on consignment and traveled out to the country to peddle the jewelry to small stores. But this enterprise was not very successful, so I decided to try something else.

I made up a Spanish course for newcomers who were arriving in greater numbers every day. I bought a book, studied it for a few days, then taught the new refugees everything I knew. The course lasted for three months, because that was all I knew by then. Then I made up a course on the Hebrew language and taught it to a group of *Hadassah* women. My next challenge was to tutor the children of the rabbi in the Torah, but the rabbi wanted me to translate into Yiddish. I did not speak Yiddish well, so the night before the lesson, a young man who spoke Yiddish fluently instructed me about the lesson for the following day. Since I had no money to pay him, I agreed to teach him all the English that I learned from a woman who lived in our building and to whom I taught exercises to strengthen her back. I juggled the classes, but when it came to payment, I was too embarrassed to ask for the money. Fortunately, I became friendly with a man named Bobek, also a recent arrival in Cuba, who was older and had some business experience, and he volunteered to collect the money for me. Still I could not scrape together enough to help with the household expenses or to buy myself some clothes, so I looked for some other ways to earn money.

My next enterprise was working for a young Hungarian Jewish refugee couple who had set up a leather shop in their apartment. Here, I put to use the skills that I had learned in Budapest. We made beautiful handbags, which they sold to stores. They made very little money, but they tried to live frugally. I was so impressed when I saw the young woman preparing their lunch, measuring out the food carefully so it would be evenly divided between the two of them, reminding me of how Anyu and I used to divide our portions equally in the camps. On special occasions she even managed to get some fruit for dessert, again carefully dividing the grapes by counting equal numbers for both plates. Of course they couldn't pay me much, and I had to find some other occupation.

Somebody offered me a job in a travel agency, downtown in old Havana. I was interviewed, and I agreed to do everything even though I was never trained for anything. The owner of the agency actually did not do much travel business but instead offered quick divorces in Haiti to Americans who lived in all parts of the United States. I typed English letters, called on the phone, arranged interviews, and minded every aspect of the office because the owner was never there. I got paid a small salary, and I felt that I was on my way to building a career.

We, the young refugees, organized a social group and named it *Brit Zionit Atid*, a Zionist fellowship. We were about 25–30 young people, girls and boys, mostly from Eastern Europe. We even decided to put on a show on the Havana Jewish Community radio program, and it was well received. I decided one day that I needed a radio of my own, and I went downtown from store to store asking if they would rent one to me, since I had no money to buy one. The merchants made fun of me, but in one of the stores the son of the owner agreed to rent one to me for $1.00 a month, but he also wanted me to go to the beach with him on Sunday. I wanted the radio very much, and I promised I would go. Sure enough, he was there the following Sunday where our group usually met. He invited me to go boating with him, and I did, but when we were out at sea, he wanted to kiss me. That was not in our agreement, so I felt justified in jumping out of the boat, which overturned, and I swam back to the shore, leaving him to his own devices. I found him in his store the next time I brought the dollar there, but he no longer asked me for a date.

One day a letter came from Mexico, and two of my uncles informed us that they were planning to visit us. Indeed, in a short time they arrived on a ship from Vera Cruz. We waited for them excitedly at the harbor. It was a joyous reunion, with much crying and expressions of gratitude. My uncle Itzu had left Hungary in 1924, at the age of 17, after his parents forbade him to buy a bicycle. He did not like the Yeshiva education that was the tradition in the family, and he single-handedly found a way to get to Mexico, against his father's wishes. He and my grandfather later reconciled. Now he came to Havana to visit us with his wife, Margit, who was also from Hungary, but they left their three children at home in Mexico.

My youngest uncle, Ali, also came with his wife, Mexican-born Graciela. Ali had also left Hungary at the age of 16, in 1938, after he could no longer stand the beatings he received from the Gentile boys in the *Levente*, the Hungarian Nationalist youth group, which was compulsory for all young men. My grandfather had already been ill and had no energy to stop his adventurous youngest son, who was also eager to escape from the strict rules of school and family. My uncle Itzu, his older brother, was already well established in Mexico and sent him the necessary papers and helped get him out. He had left on the last ship that got out of Nazi Germany, through Portugal. The third uncle in Mexico, Dave, or Dezso as we called him, did not come to visit us; perhaps he could not leave his family. He had left Hungary for Mexico when the war was already on, in 1942, and he could barely get out in time. In Mexico he married Minna Apfel, who was also a refugee from Belgium.

The visit of my uncles and aunts made a significant impression on me. This was the first time we met close family, after the destruction of the others in Europe. We tried to tell them about what happened to us and what we had learned about the death of my grandparents, uncles, aunts, and cousins. I wasn't sure that they really comprehended the enormity of the destruction. How could they? An ocean had separated us not only geographically but in terms of experiences that could not be paralleled. I looked at my Aunt Graciela, only a year older than I, dressed in a smart outfit, fashionable shoes and matching handbag—things that I had never seen before. I wondered if I would ever become like her, so self-confident and secure, whether I would ever have matching shoes and handbag.

After my uncles left, it was more difficult to put up with the hot and humid climate, the strangeness of the land, and its people where we could not fit in, the hopelessness of ever leaving Cuba. Although my uncles had reassured us that they were trying to do everything they could to get the family to Mexico, the Mexican government was still anti-Semitic and would not allow Jews to immigrate. Meanwhile Uzi and I kept a weekly correspondence, always hoping that somehow we would be together again. My friends were less convinced that this would really happen; they called Uzi the "paper fiancé." He had tried, in vain, to get me to go to Israel with him, and he had written to Anyu begging her to let me go, but she would not relent. I also had difficulty leaving her. So when the opportunity came, he decided to come to America as a student in the Jewish Theological Seminary in New York. I also decided that after almost two years of separation, we must meet again. I made up my mind to get into the United States, no matter how.

AMERICA THE BEAUTIFUL — October 1949

While I coped with life in the sweltering heat of Havana, Uzi explored the French language and culture in Paris. He had managed to get out of Hungary soon after we had left, and with the help of his friends, through Switzerland, he was able to get to France. He worked in the European office of the *Mizrachi*, the religious Zionist organization, where he was involved in the education of Jewish children, survivors of the Holocaust, and facilitated their exit from Europe to Israel.

Uzi met with most of the important leaders of the Jewish world, both from Israel and America. His boss was Dr. Josef Burg, who later became a minister in the Israeli cabinet. Although everyone knew that he wanted to settle in Israel, they also learned that his *kallah*, his fiancée, was in Cuba. So one day one of the American dignitaries suggested to Uzi that he come to America and study for the rabbinate. He promised to help Uzi gain admission to the Jewish Theological Seminary in New York, and indeed, he had followed through. Uzi did a lot of soul searching, but eventually he had given up trying to get me to go to Israel with him, and when the invitation came, he decided to make the move, with the hope that we would have a better chance of meeting again.

Uzi arrived in America in the beginning of September, 1949. He got a student visa, and he started his studies at the Seminary. He had also enrolled in the Teacher's College of Columbia University in a Master's program in mathematics. He got a job as a Hebrew teacher in Sea Gate, near Coney Island in Brooklyn. [Later, he also taught at the Central Yeshiva High School for Girls.] Thus, he was assured that he would not go hungry. Our correspondence since his arrival in America now focused on how to get me into the States. The American Consulate informed me that my visa application was rejected because the Hungarian quota was closed, due to the arrest and incarceration of Cardinal Mindszenty by the communist Hungarian government. How ironic that I couldn't get a visa to Mexico because I was Jewish, and I couldn't get into the United States because I was Hungarian. I kept corresponding with my cousin Florence Kramer in New York, asking her to investigate other possibilities of getting in. I also wrote to Uzi to keep in touch with the Kramer family and discuss the matter with them.

The young man in Havana, Itzik, who taught me Yiddish, told me one day that he heard about a pilot in the United States Air Force who smuggled people in, illegally, for $1,000. Itzik himself was interested, and said that there was another young man who had already signed up with the *macher*, the arranger. After I found out more details, I told Anyu that I had decided to go on this trip if she could get the money together. My mother was ambivalent about letting me go, but she saw that I was determined, and she knew that I really had no hope of getting together with my fiancé unless I took this chance. She borrowed and scraped to get the money together, and I made the arrangements through the pilot's "agent," a man who probably got a kickback.

The day arrived for saying goodbye to my family. I was dressed in the checkered suit that I had brought with me from Hungary. My mother gave me the money, which she made me put inside my bra. I took my toothbrush and my purse and was ready to leave. I joked with my brother about new adventures, and while I was trembling inside, I tried to reassure them that I would be safe. I told them not to expect to hear from me for a while, but that I would say my prayers and everything would turn out all right. I boarded the bus together with Itzik, and we waved through the window, but I could not see my mother and brother through my tears.

The bus left Havana, and after many hours of traveling, we arrived at the middle of the island, to a city surrounded by sugar fields. Itzik and I got two rooms in the designated hotel, and we went out to eat in a restaurant, but I could not find anything I could eat because of my *Kashrut* observance. So I chewed on some crackers I had brought with me from Havana. We got back near ten o'clock; I brushed my teeth and got ready to go to sleep in my checkered suit.

It was not long after midnight when I heard knocking on my window, and I knew that it was time to leave. A taxi was waiting for us outside; in it Itzik and I met the other young man who was to travel with us. The taxi quickly drove out of the city and soon got on a dirt road that eventually led to the vast sugar fields. We were told to get out and lie on the ground silently among the tall sugar canes. My heart was beating so loud that I was afraid it would give us away. Half an hour later we heard the humming of an airplane, circling the area, coming closer and closer, then suddenly turning around and going farther away, until it finally disappeared.

The driver ushered us quickly back into the taxi and took us back to the hotel. It appeared that the escape couldn't be carried out, but no one really explained to us what had happened. We assumed that it was not safe for the plane to land, or perhaps we were detected. We received a message that we must spend the next day in our room and get ready for the same procedure the following

149

night. Except for trying to find some food, the two young men and I stayed in the hotel, comforting and encouraging each other. They were optimistic that the next time we would get out, but I wasn't so sure. Visions of Cuban policemen, who sometimes appeared to be German soldiers, arresting us or perhaps even beating us, haunted me. I kept ruminating about my mother whom I had left, and thought that maybe I should have stayed with her and waited until my uncles could get us into Mexico.

The knock on the window came at the same time as the night before. Silently we got into the taxi, which sped off in the same direction, but it took a different dirt road, much farther away from the city. We already knew what to do when we got there—we did not need any instructions. I was shivering in my traveling clothes, even though the night was still warm. I lay on the ground and looked up at the sky. I saw the same stars that I had watched from my window back home in Miskolc when I was a child, the very same constellations that covered the sky in Auschwitz. How could it be, I wondered, that way up high everything was the same, everything was in order, but down here on earth everything was so different, so complicated and disordered?

The roar of the plane's engine jolted me back to the present. Again, the plane circled and circled endlessly. Then I saw some flares on the field and finally the plane landed a few hundred yards away. We got up and ran toward it, falling a few times in the sugar cane, but reached it at last. The pilot was a handsome blond man, dressed in a U.S. Air Force uniform, a gun in his holster, with an easy-going grin on his face. He motioned to us to get in quickly. The plane was a four-seater; I sat in the back with Itzik, and the other young man sat next to the pilot.

The plane took off in a matter of minutes, rising sharply toward the sky. I knew that I would get sick because when I was a child, I couldn't travel on any train or bus without getting sick. My grandfather used to hire Mr. Scher, who transported merchandise from Edeleny to Miskolc, and I used to get a ride with him on his horse and wagon to my home. My voyage on the ship not so long ago confirmed my problem with motion sickness. And now we were flying high, the plane bobbing from left to right and back again, which made me very nauseous. When I looked out the window and saw oil running down the wings of the plane, I got even sicker and to my embarrassment I vomited into a bag that the pilot provided. Then I gazed forward and fixed my eyes on the pilot's gun, and I became panicky. Why did he need a gun, I wondered. Would he use it on us? I did not know what my companions were thinking. Nobody spoke, nor did I utter a word.

It was daylight already when, after circling for a long while, the plane landed on an airfield somewhere in Florida. The pilot ushered us out of the plane, and I staggered into a waiting car. A woman, who turned out to be the pilot's wife, drove the car and made a quick exit. As we passed through the field, we saw some buildings and a sign "United States of America, Air Force Base."

Soon we arrived at the bungalows where servicemen lived with their families; we were asked to get inside the house quickly. The pilot's wife led us into their bathroom, reassuring us that we could come out later. The pilot changed into casual civilian clothes, and then asked for our money. My two companions complied immediately, but I hesitated. First I had to send the men out of the bathroom to retrieve the money from my bra. I had $1,000, but if I gave all of it to the pilot, how would I get to New York? I explained this to the pilot, he listened and said that he would buy me the ticket to New York; he certainly did not want me to stay behind and further endanger his position. I thanked him for his generosity.

We were all hungry, and the pilot and his wife invited us to go with them to eat. We went to a diner, not far from the base, full of servicemen. The menu offered typical American food—hamburgers, hot dogs, barbecued beef. I was very hungry, but I wouldn't order anything since it was not kosher, until the pilot insisted that I must eat the hamburger he ordered for me. He didn't want me to appear to be a foreigner, but would blend into the environment. With great difficulty I swallowed the strange food, which, predictably, upset my stomach. The pilot was in a jolly mood. He had quite a few drinks, and he sat down at the player piano and started to sing. Soon others joined in, and the place resembled a German beer hall. "My Bonnie lies over the ocean…" I heard myself imitating the words. I did not dare to stand out as a stranger. I sat on the hard chair, my body rigid with tension, expecting any minute to have men in uniform discover that I was a fugitive. I thought that the evening would never end and felt great relief when the pilot was finally ready to leave and take us to the airport. He bought my ticket as he promised under the name of Mrs. So and So, the wife of the young man, and the three of us boarded Eastern Airlines for New York. The plane hit the ground at about 5:00 a.m. at La Guardia airport. My companions had some money to hire a taxi, and they agreed to drop me off at my cousin Kramer's house in the Lower East Side of Manhattan.

It was just about daybreak on Friday morning when I knocked timidly on my cousin's door. "Oh, my God, it is Erika!" my cousin Ethel exclaimed. We hugged and kissed, and I said: "Please don't ask me how I got here." And with that I slumped down on the sofa and fell asleep. Later I asked them to try to get Uzi to come over Saturday night but not to tell him that I was already there. I wanted it to be a total surprise.

It was toward the end of October and the days were short, so I figured Uzi would be arriving from Brooklyn about an hour after Shabbat was over. I wanted to meet him alone, with no witnesses, just privately, surprising him at the subway exit. It had been almost two years since we last said goodbye to each other at the Hungarian border. During these two years, except for our weekly letters, we had had no other contact with each other, and we were not together to experience and absorb the subtle and minute changes that happen to people as they grow. I suddenly didn't remember what he looked like. I wondered if we had changed so much that we would face each other as strangers. Would the love that we promised each other back in Hungary be as strong as it had been then to overcome any perceived distance?

I stood to the side of the subway exit, and saw him come up the stairs and hurriedly turn to the right. I stepped behind him, tapped him on the shoulder and said softly: "Shalom, Uzi." He turned around and stared at me, speechless, his expression puzzled, confused. He finally said, "But how did you get here and when? How? Tell me!" Only after he recovered from the shock did we embrace, and then we looked at each other and touched each other to see if this was real or just a mirage. People were rushing by us, glancing at us as we obstructed their exit, strangers who witnessed our reunion, but they had no connection to us. We stood there a long time until I finally realized that I felt cold without a coat, and reluctantly we went back to my cousin's heated apartment and warm welcome.

After staying two weeks with my cousins, I found a furnished maid's room on Riverside Drive in uptown Manhattan in an apartment that was occupied by two refugee families. The window faced the Hudson River and in the distance I could see the George Washington Bridge majestically crossing over to New Jersey. I felt I was the luckiest girl in the world. Uzi promised to subsidize my monthly rent of $20.00, which he could save from his teacher's salary. He lived in the dormitory of the Seminary, which was about 30 blocks south of my place.

I often visited him there, but if I stayed too long, the supervising faculty would throw me out since they did not allow girls to visit there after 8:00 p.m.

I wanted to earn some money immediately, so at the suggestion of my landlord, I got a social security card under the name of Eva Heller. It felt strange to use a name that wasn't mine, but it was better than when not so long ago I was identified only by a number. I chose the name Eva, because my Hebrew name, Chava, translated to Eva; and Heller, well, because it meant in German "lighter," or maybe because it contained the word hell. I vacillated between feeling somewhat optimistic, lighter, and considering my situation worse, hellish. I found a job in Brooklyn as a sewing machine operator, working in a garment shop in the basement of a dilapidated building. I had never used a sewing machine, but if I wanted to keep the job, I had to learn how quickly. I watched how others did it and tried to imitate them, and it did not take me long to become good at it. I remembered that I learned to swim when I was a child by watching how others did it. I did not socialize at work—I did not want anyone to ask me questions.

The weather turned cool; it often rained, so after I received my first payment, I bought myself a brown coat with a rabbit collar. I thought it was beautiful. On the long subway rides to and from work, I studied "American culture." I watched what people wore, what they read, and what they ate. I learned to push myself into the crowded cars, to move away from suspicious-looking characters, to hurry on the streets, I even learned to cross the street when the light was red in order to blend in to avoid looking like I did not belong.

One Sunday Uzi and I went to the Lower East Side, and with my next paycheck, I bought 20 second-hand books that were sold on tables on the street. I arrived at my room with my treasure, and I set the books up on my little table: Virgil's Aeneid in Latin, The History of American Literature, The History of English Literature, a book on world history, the classics of Dostoyevsky and

Tolstoy, and others. Although I could not understand most of the English and certainly not the Latin, it was terribly important to me to surround myself with these books. They represented normalcy, the illusion of making up for my missed education, my wish to replace my lost home. I was happy. Now I felt that I had everything.

The view from my window was magnificent, and my salami and pickle jar, which I usually kept outside my windowsill because I had no refrigerator, kept me well fed, although sometimes I lost everything when the wind blew them down. I was sad that I could not communicate with my mother. It would have been too risky to send her, or any other member of my family, letters, and they were not able to write to me either. Anyu did not have a phone, so I could not send her a message with someone. Still, I hoped that things would improve in the future. Uzi and I spent all our free time together, getting re-acquainted, and worked hard to fill in the gaps that the distance had created.

Erika Jacoby

156

THE CHASE, OR HOW I BECAME A FUGITIVE — November 1949 to September 1950

It seemed as if my life was beginning to take on some normalcy. I had a job that paid for my food; and Uzi had a job that paid for his necessities plus my rent. We were hopeful.

Uzi kept asking me to go with him to Sea Gate, Brooklyn, for Shabbat, where he conducted Junior Congregation in the Hebrew school. I did not feel that it was proper to spend Shabbat with him, although he assured me that we would have separate rooms in the Saint Souci Lodge, a retirement home near the ocean. One day I gave in and joined him. Mrs. Moskowitz, the owner of the lodge, made me feel welcome and fed us home-cooked meals, which brought back memories of my mother's chicken soup. After Shabbat I called the landlord of my apartment, as was my custom every night before I went home. I always anticipated some trouble, and I asked if everything was okay. He and his wife were also survivors—they spoke Yiddish, but otherwise we had little in common. Although I never shared with them how I got to New York, they sensed that everything wasn't "*kosher*." Yet they were always discreet and never questioned me. This time the landlord was very brief and whispered in Yiddish, "*Nisht aheim kimmen*," meaning "don't come home." Suddenly the room closed in on me.

I called my cousins, the Kramers, to find out if they knew anything. Since I never told them the circumstances of my arrival, I just asked casually if there was anything new.

"We haven't heard from your mother," said Ethel, my cousin, "but we are sure that they are all right. By the way," she continued, "there was an article in the Yiddish newspaper about a pilot in the U.S. Air Force who was caught smuggling people from Cuba. The article mentioned that the FBI is now looking for these illegal aliens, among them some Jews, Chinese, and Communists. I am sure you have nothing to do with this, but I thought I would mention it," she said hurriedly, and hung up.

What do I do now? Where do I go? I asked myself and Uzi with a heavy heart, but there was no answer. Even though I knew the risks that I took when I embarked on this "project," I somehow naively thought that I would not have any trouble, that in America I would find protection. I wanted to believe this, after so many disappointments with countries and governments. But I had to learn, and my learning was not over.

Uzi's friends, Mayer and Esther Hershkovics, whom we had visited that evening in Brooklyn, invited me to stay overnight with them. But what to do after? I kept repeating to myself. Mayer offered to call my landlord, and he found out more.

"Two men from the FBI came today and were looking for Erika," he said. "When I told them that she left for the weekend, they searched her room. They took notes of everything that was there, they made a list of the books, letters from Uzi, an invitation to a wedding, and they found her address book and took it with them. They even opened the hem of her only skirt, which she had hanging in the closet, to see if she was hiding anything there. After much questioning, they left, but told me that I must report to them if I know anything about her. Please don't call me again, because I will get into trouble."

After much discussion, I decided that the next day I would leave town for a while. I knew only one person outside of New York; he was my former boyfriend, Shali Poll, who was now a rabbi in Trenton, New Jersey, and I called him.

"Shali, I have a problem. I must find a place to stay for a while, away from the New York area. Could I stay with you?"

"You cannot stay with me, but I am engaged to a girl from here, and I am sure that Ruth's family would invite you to their home," he said. "By the way, why do you need to leave New York? What's the problem?"

"I am sorry that I can't really talk about it, but believe me I am in trouble. Thank you for the invitation. I will take the first train in the morning."

Uzi called me every day, and his reports were very unsettling. The FBI had found out about him from my address book, and they picked him up at the Seminary and questioned him about my whereabouts. He denied that he knew where I was but agreed to cooperate with them in finding me. Then they took him into their car and asked him to lead them to all the addresses they had found in my book. They even went to the wedding that I was invited to, looking for me. After their search proved futile, they ordered Uzi to report to them immediately if he had any sign of me. Of course, the FBI did not know that Uzi had lived underground during the war, that he had rescued people without being caught, and that he would not give me away. He continued to call me on the phone to give me support and to discuss the next steps.

After a few days, I felt that I could not impose myself any longer on my friend's family, and I had to return to New York. Uzi and I agreed to meet in

Times Square; we figured that we would not be detected there among the throngs of people. We found each other and after a few anxious minutes, while watching out so we would not be discovered, we made a decision: I would contact some old friends and distant relatives in the New York area and ask each of them to put me up for one night.

And that's what I did. Again, I could not tell them why I needed a place to sleep, but everybody was kind and warm and did not ask any questions. Because I did not want them to get into trouble, in the morning I usually picked up my toothbrush and left their house. Every day I roamed the streets of Manhattan till evening. I got to like the avenues, the tall skyscrapers, the inviting store windows, and the people who were always running somewhere. I felt safe being lost among them. Every evening I arrived at the home of a different friend or relative. This went on for a while, but I was getting exhausted. The weather turned frigid, and I caught a cold and was feeling sick; I knew that I could not continue this way much longer. I could not see Uzi because he was afraid that he might be followed, and we could only communicate with each other on the phone, usually using the Hungarian or the Hebrew languages, and always with fear. We had to find another solution.

"Maybe you have to leave New York again, perhaps go to the West Coast and disappear there," he said with a shaky voice.

"But I don't know anyone there. And that would mean another long-term separation. Are you sure that our relationship would survive it?" I asked with apprehension. "There must be another way, and I'll find it."

I remembered my young Margareten cousin who had picked us up at the harbor when we arrived from Europe, back in 1947. I decided to give him a call. Until now, I had visited only friends and relatives who were also refugees, and who I felt would not betray me. I wasn't sure how my wealthy American relatives would receive me or whether I could trust them. But I knew I needed help. I was sick, and I could not walk the streets any longer. I called Fred Margareten, the young man's father, whom I remembered from my childhood when he visited us in Hungary. To my surprise, he was very kind and interested and invited me to his house for a family dinner. I went with much hesitation. The uniformed doorman and the lobby with its crystal chandeliers intimidated me. I rang the bell timidly, ready to run away, when the door opened and Fred's wife Mary received me with a friendly smile and ushered me in.

The table was set with beautiful china and silver, and the guests were already there. They greeted me, and reminded me that they remembered when I sang Hebrew songs at the family party on my way to Cuba. I was overwhelmed by their warmth, by their fancy dresses and fancy words, and I started to feel dizzy. The food was being served, food that I had not eaten for a long time, but I could not sit at the table. I excused myself and accepted the offer to rest on the sofa, because by now I had developed a fever and had a bad cough. After I revealed my problem to them, the family decided that I needed to see two other cousins, one who was a doctor and another one, a lawyer.

Dr. Isidore Margaretten was a neurologist, a dignified, European-style older man, a second cousin of my mother. He gave me a thorough checkup and reassured me that it was just a bad cold and nothing serious. "Bed rest," he ordered, "and don't go out in this terrible weather." I was too embarrassed to tell him that I had no bed to rest in, that the street was my home now, but thanked him profusely for his advice.

My next task was to contact Jacob I. Horowitz, the other second cousin, who was an attorney. He made an appointment with me and Uzi. We told him about my situation, and after a long discussion with us, he recommended that I give myself up. He was sure that eventually the FBI would find me even if I left town. "The FBI has long arms," an expression I took literally but was too timid to ask its meaning. "I will contact the FBI and find out what would happen to you if you gave yourself up. I am sure you would be arrested, but if they require bail for your release, I will secure that from the family."

The day came when I met my cousin in his office, and together with his son Jerry, who was also an attorney, we appeared at the offices of the FBI. I was shivering, not just from the cold but from the anticipation of what was coming. The hearing took place soon after we arrived. After many hours of questioning, I was handcuffed and led into another room. A female officer accompanied me to the restroom and then offered me something to drink. Toward the end of the day, I was called back to the room, and the person in charge of the interrogation said:

"You are a lucky girl. Many of the people who were smuggled in a similar way were Chinese or Communists, and when the pilot was in danger of detection, he would shoot them and drop them into the ocean."

"But I am not a Communist." I remembered my narrow escape from my Communist boss in Hungary.

"We have to be sure that you are not a Communist, so we have to keep track of your whereabouts at all times until your deportation."

I froze when I heard the word "deportation." How could it be that here, again, I would be sent away, deported?

"Deportation?" I gasped. "Where to?" I asked, the words almost inaudible.

"It depends what country will take you in. We can always send you back to Cuba, but then again it may be Hungary or Germany or Japan, the countries that lost the war, that have to take you in."

My cousin Jacob I. Horowitz tried to calm me down and told me that he had secured bail for me, and that I would be released for the present time and would not be put in jail. I would have to send in a report every month and wait for further instruction.

I returned to my rented room after weeks of wandering. I arranged and re-arranged the books on my desk, and then looked out the window. I saw the bare trees of the Palisades across the Hudson River, the busy George Washington Bridge, the cars, and the people on Riverside Drive walking their dogs. Yes, everything was there; the world did not stop. Only I was immobilized, unable to make sense of my life, not knowing where my road would take me. I don't know how long I stayed in this stupor, but suddenly I was jolted back to my senses when the pickle jar in my window fell crashing down to the street below. Fortunately it did not hit anyone, and it helped me to pull myself together. I took a few deep breaths and I felt lighter. I said to myself that after all, I was free now, I had my own bed, and I had my books. The next day I would see Uzi, and we would figure out something.

I was resolved to continue my life as if I had a right to stay in the U.S. I enrolled in a business school to learn some skills that could help me earn a living. The school placed me at a firm as an apprentice clerk; I earned $13 a week, from which I had to pay the school $9. I still had enough money left to buy a hot dog every day for lunch and something for dinner. After I finished the course, the school found a job for me as a bookkeeper at Strout Realty in Manhattan. When I was interviewed and was asked how much experience I had, I said two years, as my teacher at the school had instructed me.

"If you told the truth, you would never be hired," he assured me. "You know as much as anyone who has worked for two years, and you have life experience that counted more."

I was hired. My salary was $40 a week, and I felt as if I had won the lottery.

Every month I received a notice to appear at the FBI offices, ready for deportation. Every month my cousin Jacob I. Horowitz, the attorney, sent in another excuse as to why I could not be deported at that time. But eventually he could not help me any more and suggested that I hire another attorney, one who specialized in immigration. He recommended Mr. Ypsilanty, whose reputation was impeccable, and his fee was sky high. I managed to borrow the money from relatives and friends and started my long odyssey toward legalization. The plan was that after Uzi and I got married, he would find a job as a professor, and he would apply to become a permanent resident under the McCarren Bill. He then could bring me in as his wife. However, we were warned that the McCarren Bill would expire by December 25th, 1952, and that all this had to be accomplished before that date.

I met another cousin, Rabbi Edward Horowitz, and he offered to help. He, his wife, Silvia, and their children became our mentors and friends, and taught us all about the intricacies of American life. They suggested that the first thing to do was to get married. They offered us a home in their basement, and the rabbi married us in their living room on September 24th, 1950. We chose the date because it was the day before the holiday of *Sukkoth,* which came just a few days after the Jewish high holidays. Since I had already taken three days off for *Rosh Hashanah* and *Yom Kippur*, I was afraid to ask for more days off for *Sukkoth.* We thought a wedding would be a legitimate reason to miss work rather than telling my boss that we had another Jewish holiday. I worked in an all-Gentile office, and I could not imagine that it was possible to stay out of work for another Jewish holiday, that I would not be fired or punished some other way for my Jewish observance.

We wanted only a few close people to be at the wedding, especially since neither my mother nor our siblings could get visas, or had the money to come.

But Eddy, my cousin the rabbi, insisted: "You must invite a lot of people so you get lots of gifts and get a good start in your life together." Another lesson to learn; we agreed and started our preparations. Uzi had a cousin, Malka, who got married a month before our wedding, so I borrowed her wedding dress, which she had also borrowed from someone else. I could not afford the ten dollars for the cleaning of the dress, but I still had time, I thought. So I waited. The following week there was a once a year "Special" at the Thrift-De-Lux cleaner for wedding gowns. It looked like the heavens were smiling on me, and I had my gown cleaned for 99 cents.

We got married in my cousin's living room at 1334 Carroll Street, in the Crown Heights section of Brooklyn. We descended the staircase that led from their bedrooms to the main floor to the tune of the traditional wedding march, played on a record player that was set up in the dining room. Since we had no parents there, Regina Margareten and Uzi's Aunt Esther led me to the *huppa*.(the wedding canopy). They were supposed to give me support, but it was I who had to hold on to the two elderly ladies so they would not fall down the steps. Uzi walked in stiffly, accompanied by Fred Margareten and my Uncle Hermush, who had arrived in America a few weeks before. Anyu, who was already living in Mexico, called just before the ceremony and gave me her emotional blessing. Some of the invited guests were friends and distant relatives from Hungary; some we met just then for the first time. After the ceremony, we moved down to the basement for the reception. My cousin Silvia prepared cold cuts and salads and even a wedding cake. We ate and drank and sang Hebrew songs, songs of joy and celebration.

When everyone had left, we folded the tables and chairs, helped clean up the place, and retired to our new home, in the basement. We received enough money gifts to cover the expenses of the wedding, and to pay the photographer so we could send pictures to my mother. The next day I bought myself a navy blue pleated dress and pair of old fashioned, sturdy brown shoes.

We had no money left for a real honeymoon, but my former boyfriend, Shali, who was already married at that time, came to our aid again and invited us to spend the two days of the holidays in Trenton as guests of him and his wife. We were able to distance ourselves from our problems for a few days. After we returned to Brooklyn and went back to work, it seemed as if we were just another ordinary couple of newlyweds. My cousins had an extensive library and I started to read books in English. I felt truly accomplished.

෴

HOW TO BECOME AN AMERICAN —
October 1950 to December 1952

The monthly reporting to the FBI and the monthly payments to the attorney kept us on our toes, and wore our nerves thin. We couldn't make plans because every month the order of deportation hung over my head. I never knew if I would be able to stay in the U.S.

I continued my work at Strout Realty where eventually they found out that I had arrived in America only a relatively short time before. I worried that they would send me away, but they liked my work and I stayed. Working at this large real estate company, with offices coast to coast, I was introduced to many aspects of this country that I couldn't have learned about so quickly otherwise: the hierarchy of the business world, the power of advertising, even the geography of the United States. But as a Jewish girl in an all-Christian environment, I never felt that I was part of the crowd, even though they always treated me with kindness. At Christmas time to my delight and surprise, I even got a bonus, but I did not understand why every time I happened to be under the mistletoe, someone wanted to kiss me. Finally, I hid in the restroom to escape. Thus I was slowly learning the "American Way."

Uzi continued his studies at the Seminary and at Columbia University, as well as his work in Sea Gate, so we managed our daily lives adequately. Finally, through a family member, he was offered a job as a professor in a boarding school outside of New York, which would give him permission to stay in the country after his student visa expired. This was a very promising development and we hoped that through him, I would also be able to get a visa at a future time.

We lived in the basement of the Horowitzes' home, and we learned about American culture and customs from them and tried to fit in. My cousin, Silvia, even taught me to accept gifts graciously, rather than object when someone wanted to give me something. Their family accepted us and made us feel welcome. Somehow it was difficult for us to believe that we really had a right to enjoy life. After living a year in the basement, we had the good luck of finding a little apartment a couple of blocks away from my cousins. We moved in and were ready for the arrival of our first baby in December, 1952.

Meanwhile Anyu and my brother, Zoli, were able to get into Mexico with my uncles' help, and had started their new life there. Zoli was working with the uncles, and in 1951 he got married to Fruma Rappaport, and later had two children, Adriana and Jorge. Anyu was desperately longing to see us, and finally, in November, 1952, she got permission to visit us. It had been three years since I had last seen her, the longest time we had ever been away from each other, so it was a very emotional reunion. She didn't care much for our apartment and criticized the modest furniture we had acquired, because compared to my uncles' homes in Mexico, we lived like paupers. She expected that in America every home would be spacious and beautiful, and she wished that her only daughter had the best of everything. I felt hurt, but instead of telling her, I reminded her how far we had come and admonished her: "Things are just things—one day we have it and the next day it's gone. Don't you remember?"

Our baby arrived three weeks early. My doctor was not available for the delivery since I belonged to HIP, a managed care organization, and a different doctor was on call that night. I was in a giant hospital, no familiar faces around me, and I was very scared. The baby weighed less than five pounds and was considered premature; the umbilical cord was wrapped around his neck when he was delivered. His name on the birth certificate was Ronald Yakov. I only saw him once when they wheeled me to the nursery; he was a tiny creature, pale, yellowish skin, and big eyes. I wanted so much to hold him but they said it was against the rules. I returned to my room, crying and disappointed. On the third day following his birth, when Uzi and my mother came to visit, I saw on their faces that something was wrong. Soon the doctor arrived and told us that the baby had died the night before. He could not give us a reason for the baby's death and said that only if they performed an autopsy could they know more. I refused the autopsy and had the baby buried in a Jewish cemetery.

I went home and mourned my baby as I folded and unfolded baby clothes every day. The death of our first child catapulted us back in time to the heartaches of other losses, of overwhelming self doubts. Again, we questioned whether we would ever have a normal life.

We did not have enough time to grieve, because we knew that I had only a month to leave the country for Canada and reenter the United States legally.

Because earlier Uzi had gotten a position as a professor in the Roosevelt School in Hyde Park, he could gain permanent entry to the U.S. under the McCarren Bill. He had picked up his visa in Canada, and now, our lawyer told us, he had a right to bring in his wife. I also had to go to Montreal, Canada, to pick up my visa. But there was a problem: the Canadians would not give me permission to enter that country unless I already had a re-entry permit to the U.S. I could not get a re-entry permit because I was under order of deportation.

Finally, through many connections and additional attorney fees, literally at the last minute, a special bill was introduced in the Congress, giving me a re-entry permit. Now I was ready to go; there was very little time. The McCarren Bill would expire on Christmas day, the 25th of December, 1952, and I had only one day to travel to Montreal and pick up my visa. It had been only four weeks since the birth and loss of my baby, and I was shaky as I boarded the plane for Montreal on the 23rd of December.

I spent the night at the house of a distant relative. I woke up early in the morning and waited anxiously for my friend from Hungary, Ervin Schwartz, to accompany me to the American Consulate. The sky was overcast; the cold Arctic wind took my breath away as we approached the Consulate. I was sure that something would go wrong, but I picked up my visa without any problem. I held the document in my hand—I did not believe it was real. I expected something dramatic to follow, bells ringing, a celebration, but it was just an ordinary event, a window, a clerk, and a rubber stamp.

The weather had turned even worse, but we managed to take the bus to the airport. As I stood at the ticket counter, I was informed that due to the snowstorm, all flights were cancelled for that day. Again the cold vise of despair grabbed my heart. But my friend Ervin thought that we could still get to the railroad station, and that there might be a train that would cross the border before midnight. That was my only chance to enter the U.S. before the visa expired. We searched the schedule and talked to the stationmaster, and finally, I found a train that would cross the border at 11:45 p.m. that night. I said goodbye to my friend and boarded the train, clutching my ticket, with my visa in my hand.

It was a slow moving, local train which stopped at every little town and village; I wished that I had the power to push the engine faster, but to no avail. At 11:45 p.m. the train stopped at the American border, and the U.S. Immigration

Officer entered the cabin. "Tickets and documents, please," he said, nonchalantly, and took them from my shaking hands. Then, as if by a magic that only I understood, he stamped the visa with the seal of the United States, and with the date and time of entry.

There was no host of angels singing hosannas. Only I was there, alone, with the impersonal train that pulled out of the station with deliberate slowness, as if everything could be turned around and the mirage could disappear. I looked out the window and saw white snowflakes falling swiftly by. The sky was dark, no stars were visible, and the bare trees were reaching their branches toward me. I wanted to hug the whole world.

Erika Jacoby

A "NORMAL" LIFE — New York–Los Angeles

My mother returned to Mexico and I returned to work. I packed up the baby clothes and gave them away. Although the doctor reassured me that there was no reason why I couldn't have another baby, it was hard for me to believe him. I heard from other refugees that it was common for survivor women to lose their first babies because of the drug bromide we had been given in the camps and because of the physical deprivation. But a glimmer of hope remained inside me that maybe the doctor was right. I had been in many seemingly irremediable and gloomy situations before, and still things had turned around. And I reminded myself of the miracle that I had just experienced, the miracle that finally I was a free person, an American, with rights and privileges, and I must be thankful for that. And I prayed. My second pregnancy was uneventful.

I went to Uzi's graduation from Columbia University where he received a Master's degree in teaching mathematics. He also graduated from the Jewish Theological Seminary with the degrees of Master in Hebrew Education and Bachelor of Divinity. With his diplomas in hand, we were ready to embark on a new adventure. As a recent graduate, he was invited by the Valley Jewish Community Center and Temple (VJCC), a large Conservative synagogue in

North Hollywood, California, to become the principal of its Hebrew School. We packed our bags, borrowed $400 for the move, and took the train to Los Angeles. We arrived after three days of travel, on July 15th, 1953. We rented an apartment, our furniture and our books arrived, the weather was beautiful, the people friendly. Still, I had a hard time feeling at home. I complained that there were not enough trees in North Hollywood. I ached to belong somewhere; I was homesick, but I did not know what place I was longing for. No place was my home.

Our son was born on October 21st, 1953, a year after the loss of our first baby, and we named him Jonathan David, Yakov David in Hebrew, after my father who perished in the Holocaust and Uzi's grandfather, who died before the Holocaust in Hungary, at a ripe old age. Jonathan was a healthy baby, he developed nicely, and we treasured him. To us he was a miracle, a special gift from God—as his name indicated.

Anyu was able to come and stay with us for a few weeks, and she came back again the following year. During her visit in 1954 she became ill and had to be hospitalized. She was diagnosed with infectious hepatitis, which she had picked up in Mexico through an infected needle when she was treated for vitamin B12 deficiency. Soon she fell into a coma, her liver was completely gone, and the doctors had given up on her. I was devastated, I couldn't accept that after having lived through the Holocaust, we would lose her this way. My uncle Hermush and my brother Zoli flew in, and we spent every minute by her side, praying for her recovery. We called in a famous specialist from UCLA, who suggested that we try massive doses of cortisone. After two weeks in a coma, my mother suddenly regained consciousness. "It was a miracle, plain miracle," Doctor Feinfield, her physician, repeated. "It was your prayers that brought her back."

Parenting became the most important task in my life. Although I tried to be a relaxed mother, when something happened that threatened the safety or the well-being of my child, it became difficult to control my anxiety. Every incident that others perhaps might take in stride, every separation, brought back painful memories and held me hostage for a while.

When Jonathan was two years old, he was injured when an older child knocked him down and rode a bicycle over him; he suffered a concussion. He was hospitalized then, and again, every time his symptoms returned. The hospital policy had allowed the parent to stay with the child only during visiting hours. Saying goodbye to him every time we left was traumatic for him and for us. When he finally recovered, it took us a while to overcome our tendency to overprotect him.

Our second son arrived on April 13th, 1956, on a sunny Friday morning, and he was named Benjamin Mark, Binyamin Zev in Hebrew, after Uzi's father and my paternal grandfather, both murdered in Auschwitz. He was a lively, beautiful baby who won the hearts of everyone with his dimples and blond curls. But, as if to remind us of the fragile nature of normalcy, after he was weaned, he stopped gaining weight and had chronic diarrhea. After months of tests, he was diagnosed with celiac disease. We finally gained control of the illness by following a very strict, special diet that he had to maintain for years, and slowly he got better. But he was never allowed to eat the cookies that his older brother had secretly given him.

Our youngest son, Michael Don, came fourteen months later, on July 5th, 1957, and he got my younger brother's Hebrew name, Moshe, who was only 15 when he was shot to death just days before the liberation. Yosef, his Hebrew middle name, was the name of my maternal grandfather, who was killed in the Holocaust. Michael was a sweet, easygoing child, but he also had celiac disease. Fortunately, by then we were able to handle it more calmly, and his good nature and sweet face rewarded us with happiness. And with that our family was complete.

The birth of our children helped us to stabilize our lives, to establish a home, to become part of a community, and nurture our feelings of belonging. When we became American citizens, we changed our names officially from Jakubovics to Jacoby. And one day I bought myself a lavender kerchief.

Uzi worked at Valley Jewish Community Center and Temple, later called Adat Ari El, for 23 years as its Education Director. After a successful career there, he took on the position of Associate Director of the Bureau of Jewish Education of Los Angeles, and in 1983 became its Executive Director. Again, he accomplished a great deal in both of these positions and created a good name for himself in the educational community. Concurrently he also taught at the University of Judaism, and directed the Hebrew educational program at Camp Ramah, in Ojai, where our family had spent 15 glorious summers, from 1961 through 1976. After he retired as Executive Director of the Bureau of Jewish Education in 1993, he established a school accreditation program at the Bureau and is still directing it.

I filled my life with raising the children, playing in the mud with them, making peanut butter and jelly sandwiches, learning American folk songs from their records, and making friends with the parents of their friends. On Sundays I taught Hebrew school, and during the week I took classes at the University of Judaism.

After the birth of Michael, Anyu moved to the United States permanently. She lived with us, helped around the house, and wanted to take over the raising of the children, which I fought fiercely. Eventually she found a job as a cook and a dietitian in a nursing home in the city, and she stayed with us only on her days off until she retired in 1963 at the age of 62.

When our children started school, my neighbor, Jerry Silver, urged me to enroll at Valley College. Because I had not been able to go even to high school in Hungary, I thought that I could never get into a college or university. But finally, after years of longing for a higher education, this dream had also become a reality. After Valley College, I went to California State University (CSUN), where I received a Bachelor of Arts degree and then went on to the University of Southern California (USC) where I got a Master's degree in clinical social work. It took me eleven years to reach this goal. I could not have done it without Uzi's encouragement and cooperation and Anyu's help in the house and her sharing with me her social security money for two years. When I graduated, I gave her and Uzi diplomas for all the support they had given me.

I was very happy with the profession I had chosen. It gave me satisfaction to be able to help people resolve their problems, overcome their difficulties, and to see them grow. My first job as a clinical social worker was at Family Service of Los Angeles, where I worked for five years and two summers, and then got a position at Kaiser Psychiatry where I spent 17 exciting and fulfilling years. My clientele included families, individuals, and children; I specialized in the treatment of trauma and grief. Among my clients were many survivors and their children who were struggling with the effects of the Holocaust, its trauma, and their losses. I decided to retire in 1997 from Kaiser because Anyu's physical and mental condition had deteriorated to the point that I spent the major part of my days taking care of her needs, and I could not continue full-time employment. I have been maintaining a private practice in my home, and that keeps me involved with my profession.

Our sons left the family home and have not lived with us since they started their university educations. Although I never verbalized it, I must have given them permission to leave and not feel obligated to stay near us, and to be so totally attached to their parents the way many second-generation children were, and the way I was with my mother. When I am especially lonely, though, it is hard to hold on to feeling good about giving them the gift of freedom that I never had, and I wish I could have held them close, but not chained.

Our sons are all married. Jonathan, our oldest, graduated from UCLA and from the University of Judaism. He got a Master's degree at Harvard University in education. He lives in New York and is married to Donna Bojarsky, of Los Angeles; they have a bi-coastal marriage. Last year Donna gave birth to a son, Joshua, our tenth grandchild. Jonathan also has a 16-year-old son, Jesse, from his first marriage to Evelyn Sucher. Jonathan has always been a community activist. Starting as a high school student when he organized rallies for the Soviet Jews, at UCLA where he was among the founders of the *"BAYIT,"* and started *"HAAM,"* a Jewish student newspaper. In Israel, he worked with *"Shutfut,"* a group of Israeli Jews and Arabs trying to create communication between them and joint projects. He has spent most of his adult life as founder and director of numerous organizations, starting with the New Israel Fund, then Americans for Peace Now, and for the past 10 years, he has been with the Israel Policy Forum, always working for peace in Israel. His wife Donna is the daughter of Sol and Celina Bojarski, who have both been active in the Jewish community. Donna enjoys her new role as a mother, but she also continues to be a tireless community worker and has been involved with many political and philanthropic organizations.

Benjamin has always combined his interest in sports and nature with serious Jewish learning. After he graduated from Rambam High school, he spent 12 years in Israel, studying to become an Orthodox rabbi. He is the disciple of Rabbi Wolbe, the great *"Musar"* (ethical) scholar, in Beer Yakov, and he received his ordination there and in *Kollel Chazon Ish,* in Bnei Brak. He and his family made their home in Toronto, Canada, where he works for *Ohr Sameach,* JEP, an outreach organization. He gives classes for Jewish students at universities and at his home, where he not only teaches them, but he and his family welcome them to their table on Shabbat and holidays. He is also the unofficial counselor of his community where young people and sometimes their parents turn to him for advice, regarding relationships, marriage, and parent-child problems. He is married to Etta Sugarman, the daughter of Rabbi Marvin and Avis Sugarman, of Valley Village. Etta, besides teaching remedial classes, is a faithful partner to Benjie in his work with young people. They have five children—Shalom Tzvi, 20, Shaina, 18, Doovie, 16, Yaacov, 14, and Simha, seven.

Michael married Cary Ehrenberg of Evanston, Illinois, the daughter of Maxine. Her father died when Cary was an infant, and Maxine successfully raised her three children. Michael also spent a year in a Yeshivah in Israel, but instead of staying there, he came back and went to college. He graduated from Sarah Lawrence in New York and learned about the diamond business while he was a student there; this continues to be his occupation. He and Cary met in Israel, where Cary was finishing her Master's degree at the Hebrew University. For a while they lived in Chicago, then in 1994 they announced that they would be moving to Israel. When we asked why they decided to move there, Michael said: "Isn't it what you always wanted to do? So now we move there instead of you." They live in Tzur Hadassah, a small community outside Jerusalem, within the "Green Line," and they are well integrated there. Cary teaches English and volunteers with the aged blind. Cary and Michael were instrumental in founding their synagogue in Tzur Hadassah, which is affiliated with the Progressive Judaism movement in Israel. They have three children, Ariel, 15, Ben, 13, and Yael, nine.

We spend all our vacations visiting our children in the three countries where they live, and they also come to Los Angeles, separately and together, to spend time with us and to celebrate special events. We have good relationships with all our children, and we delight and rejoice in our grandchildren.

In spite of what I had gone through or maybe because of it, I feel I have been blessed. I have a wonderful, supportive husband, who has been by my side through both joys and heartbreak. We raised our sons to be good, responsible, and sensitive people, loyal to their heritage. When they were young, we tried to give them the freedom to grow and establish their own identity. I often refer to them, jokingly, as being in the "repair business": Jonathan, our oldest, wants to repair the world; Benjamin, our second, works to repair the Jews; our youngest, Michael, concentrates on repairing his mother.

During these 50 years in North Hollywood, California, now Valley Village, I have been living a full and rewarding life. For the last 40 years, I have been speaking about the Holocaust and worked with other survivors, professionally, as well as informally. Although I also do additional volunteer work, nothing feels as satisfying as knowing that sharing my experiences as a survivor may contribute in some way to bringing about a better world for future generations.

AFTERTHOUGHTS

MY MOTHER, "ANYU"

It has now been 58 years since I was liberated from the concentration camp. Many mental health practitioners have asserted that the effect of such trauma is long lasting—perhaps one never really recovers from it. In my practice as a clinical social worker, I often treated Holocaust survivors who suffered from post-traumatic stress disorder. Some made considerable improvement, others will never recover. Even if one made much progress in adjusting to "normal" life, the Holocaust remains an eternal wound, or at least a major reference point, to most of us. I cannot have an encounter with members of my family or with friends when we don't automatically go back to our experiences during WWII, even if the occasion is a happy one. It has become a binding fellowship, as it may be true among others who have gone through a common experience.

I often wonder if I am psychologically healthier than many other survivors are, and if I am, then I ask myself to what I owe this. Perhaps it is because my experiences were not as horrendous as those of other survivors from countries such as Poland and Czechoslovakia who had spent longer periods in the camps. Or perhaps it is because I was able to keep my faith during and after the Holocaust. But the explanation that sounds most real is that I survived with

Anyu, my mother. I knew in the camps that I would not give up and become a *Musulman*, one who lost all will to live, because I had to stay alive for my mother. I had to take care of her—I couldn't let her lose another child.

This "duty to stay alive for her" also determined our relationship in the years following the war, with both positive and negative consequences. This memoir would not be complete if I did not look at this relationship that has changed from what it had been before the war.

When I was a child, back in Miskolc, my mother had always been a strong independent woman, dedicated to the business, totally devoted to her own father whom she idealized and idolized. She believed in discipline and self-discipline, and we all had to obey the rules. Bedtime had never varied, at nine o'clock the lights were turned off, and there were no exceptions. We looked up to her as the one who would always find a solution to a problem. Anyu was brave. It was she, my mother, who would grab a butcher knife if some anti-Semitic hoodlums tried to break into our restaurant. But she was just marginally involved with me; she left my care to others, although I always knew that she was there, which gave me a sense of security. My most pleasant memories with my mother were when she shared with me her childhood experiences, her interest in historical events and nature. I felt especially privileged when she gave me the books she had received in school for academic excellence when she was a student in the Catholic middle school she had attended.

But things changed during the concentration camp and after that. In the camps I discovered that my mother could not save me from all the suffering; indeed, she could no longer take care of herself. I became *her* protector—I saw her as powerless. After the war she had acquired a different kind of power, a power that I had given her. From the time that we returned home to the very day Anyu died in 1998, she had become very dependent on me. Although on the outside she appeared strong and self-confident, and although she never admitted it, she felt insecure without my presence in her life all the time. Indeed, she never established her own separate identity in America, because in a new country with a new language, she needed me to become her interpreter, her guide, and her emotional provider.

She never remarried, in spite of the many opportunities that arose throughout the years. Even the man whom she had wanted to marry before she had met my father and who survived the war and wanted to marry her, she declined. She lived with us for many years, refusing to have her own, separate place. When finally we suggested that we find her an apartment close to our home, she developed an "acute stress reaction." Her body became rigid, she refused food or drink for days, did not respond to anyone who talked to her. Only with professional help did she come out of it. Although it was never verbalized, it became a law in our family that my mother's needs were primary. My own desires, wishes, even those of my husband and of my children, became only secondary. I felt I had no choice. I was convinced that it was my responsibility to provide her with everything. Consciously or unconsciously, I took it upon myself to give meaning to her life, to compensate her for her losses, in short, to make her happy—an impossible task that many survivors who had parents, and especially the children of survivors, have tried, unsuccessfully.

This somewhat symbiotic relationship affected my own development. During my adolescence, teenage rebellion was unknown to me, and later as a young adult, the right to separate and exclude my mother from the intimacy of my new family filled me with guilt. The freedom to give expression to my own feelings and thoughts, that might be in opposition to hers, caused me anxiety and tension, so I would avoid it, and so did Uzi and our children. I was always conflicted when we went out at night and left her at home; she often acted like an abandoned child, or at least that's how I perceived it. Many of my friends recognized this bind and would often invite her with us, and I would feel relieved, though somewhat embarrassed. I did not feel that I had a right to seek help; after all, I should be grateful that I had a mother, as other survivors often reminded me. Therapy would have meant betrayal. But finally, I did go to see someone when I felt that for my children's sake I needed to assert myself and do what I thought was proper and right.

But my relationship with Anyu has also given me many positives. She was a tireless and devoted parent who would be there to help me any time I needed it, and, indeed, even when I didn't need it. She cooked and baked and gardened in my home; she became famous for her culinary skills. Our children looked up to her and learned from her perseverance and courage. My extended family and my friends were in awe of her intellect and her strength—indeed, she was loved by all, but also feared by some as well. Her faith had remained steadfast throughout her life and had influenced our lives in staying true to our traditions. Anyu was often angry, angry for all her losses, for the shattered dreams. She would openly express her rage against the Nazis, the Hungarians, and the Germans, something I could never do. So, just as I took care of her needs, she gave voice to my own repressed negative feelings.

Anyu had often made me promise that I would never put her in a nursing home when she became old and feeble, a promise I kept till the end. Although I was tempted to place her in a home during the last year of her life, when she became obsessed by phantom persecutors and accused me of trying to poison her, I could not do it. During the last months of her life, it was as if she became another person, one she despised, couldn't accept. She wanted me around all the time, but still she could not reconcile to her diminished self. She wanted me to figure out her thoughts and feelings, when she could not express them, and she became angry with me if I failed. She could not comprehend that I would not think and feel what she did.

The day before Anyu died, she was especially agitated. I took her in my arms and said to her quietly that it was all right with me if she wanted to leave me, that I loved her very much, but I did not want her to suffer any more. She relaxed and let her body go. Then she said this last word to me in Hungarian: *kegyelem,* which translated could mean forgiveness, or mercy. I don't know whose forgiveness she was seeking—perhaps God's. The next day she died in my arms, in her own bed, at age 96. When the mortuary van took her away, I ran after her. I couldn't bear her leaving me. This was a most painful, unnatural experience, as if something was torn out of my insides, tearing, cutting, bleeding, perforating. I tried to let go of Anyu, not just of her, but also of my father, my grandparents, brother, aunts, uncles, and cousins whose deaths we never really mourned

On the first anniversary of her death, I went for a walk early in the morning, smelled the flowers, and I wanted to tell her how beautiful everything was. That's what I missed most: to tell her about the lilacs and the lily of the valley which bloomed when we were in Toronto; and the many flowering trees in Israel, when we were there on Passover; and the newly planted tulips in the middle of Broadway, when we visited Jonathan. I picked some ripe tomatoes and gave them to my friends, saying: "These are gifts from Anyu." Then I sat in her yellow chair and waited for her to step out of the patio door.

Erika Jacoby

REVISITING THE PAST

As the years passed, the details of my experiences started to fade. I had written down everything I remembered years before, but somehow I felt that I needed to go back, physically, to *that* place again, to touch the walls of the barracks, to see the railroad tracks, even to smell that awful disinfectant. In May of 1978 Uzi and I met our youngest son, Michael, who had just graduated from college, and we traveled from New York to Vienna. There we were joined by our sons, Jonathan and Benjie, who were both studying in Israel at the time. We rented a car and embarked on a trip to Eastern Europe, a trip of recovery in every sense of the word.

It was very important to us to have our children with us on this trip. We needed to reassure ourselves that our lives had indeed turned around, that what we were going to see and experience all belonged to our past. We also wanted to be sure that our sons understood our history, our own as well as that of the Jewish people, especially since, besides my mother, there were no other grandparents to tell them stories about it.

From Vienna we traveled to Hungary first. We spent a few days in Budapest and searched out the places where our families had lived and where Uzi had hidden and worked in the underground during the war. Then we went to Miskolc, where I tried to recapture my childhood. I visited my old home, the schools that I had attended, the synagogue, and the village, Edeleny, where my grandparents had lived. Everything seemed as though I was walking in a dream—there were no acquaintances, no friends or family we could talk to. I felt distant like a stranger; I felt no connection to the people. Then we visited our old maid, Mari. She had prepared my favorite childhood drink that we used to call "bird's milk," and which brought back forgotten memories. An overwhelming feeling of sadness replaced the feelings of nothingness, of emptiness. After we dried our eyes, I was ready to leave the place and continue our journey toward Auschwitz.

We passed through towns and villages where Jews had once lived, and we looked for abandoned synagogues and cemeteries everywhere. Sometimes we found some Jews who were excited by our presence, and often with our family, they were able to make a *minyan*, a quorum of ten that is required for public prayer. When we arrived in Krakow, Poland, we stayed in the apartment of a young Polish couple who rented rooms. We had difficulty communicating with them because they spoke only Polish and a little bit of German. They had never met Jews before, so they said, and looked at us with suspicion when we declined to eat with them the ham and cheese they prepared and, instead, we opened the cans of tuna and ate the matzos we had brought with us. Then we lit a *Yahrzeit* candle because it was the eve of the anniversary of the death of Uzi's family. Uzi and the boys sat on the mattresses on the floor and studied *Mishnayot*, holy books, as was customary to do when one had *Yahrzeit*. The couple just looked on questioningly. Only when we were leaving the next day and asked for directions to Auschwitz was there a sign of recognition on their faces that, perhaps, they made the connection between Jews and Auschwitz.

Auschwitz was only about 50 miles west of Krakow, and we arrived there early in the morning. We passed through the gate above which the sign "*Arbeit Macht Frei*," which translates as "Work Makes One Free," still appears. Then we went to see the exhibits, the different barracks, the windows of tattered suitcases that the prisoners brought with them, the mountains of shoes, of eyeglasses, of human hair that were collected from the exterminated. We saw nowhere any mention that Jews were murdered there, only so many Poles, Hungarians, Russians, Czechoslovaks, and others. We walked around in a frozen state, silent, disconnected. We followed a group that was led by an English-speaking guide, and suddenly my numbness changed into rage. I listened to what the guide said, and then I interrupted him and asked, trembling: "Why is there no mention of the six million Jews who were annihilated in the Holocaust, the millions who were gassed and incinerated in Auschwitz?" My children looked at me; they had never seen me so angry. The members of the group turned around, among them the daughter of Kurt Waldheim, who was then the President of Austria, and heard the guide answer: "We list the people by their nationalities, not by their religion."

"But," I said, "my father, my brother, my grandparents were not murdered because they were Hungarians—they were killed because they were Jews." To which the guide turned away and the group continued the tour. I was frustrated and angry but also almost grateful that after years of hiding my anger, finally I had the opportunity to release it. It was a liberating feeling, and it also signified that I was no longer so traumatized by the experience that I was afraid to express my anger.

Then someone directed us to the "Jewish Pavilion," which we found out had always been kept locked. When after much fuss they opened it for us, a young Polish woman wanted to take us around. I told her that we did not need a guide, that I had been there as a prisoner, and we wanted our privacy. We had planned our travel to Auschwitz exactly for the day that Uzi's parents were deported and killed there. Here, in this Jewish Pavilion, with the piped-in, melancholy sounds of the *Yisgadal*, the closest place to where our families were lost, we gathered around the memorial candle that flickered in a glass case. We held on to each other and wept. Together we stood there and recited the *Kaddish*.

In Birkenau, three miles away from Auschwitz, I found the place where my barrack had been but which only had its chimney still standing. In another barrack I showed the wooden platforms to the other visitors around me. There were three planks lined up on top of each other that served as our beds; on each plank 10 of us had been plastered together. After that we proceeded to the barrack that had housed the latrine, the two rows of holes where our social life had taken place, and where my Aunt Lilli had fallen in one night. I searched for the swimming pool of the Nazi officers where, at the risk of my life, I had jumped in and swum across, but I could not find it. Finally, I saw the entrance to the gas chamber and the ovens of the crematoria; we stood as if in a nightmare, unable to move. When I felt my blood circulating in my body again, I bent down and picked two daisies that grew wild from the side of the hill above them. We looked at the railroad tracks that led to Birkenau and the memorials that had been erected to all the nations. Not one of them mentioned the Jews. There were no words coming to our lips, but our minds felt as though they would explode.

On our way out, through Auschwitz again, I used the restroom. The same odor of the disinfectant that the Nazis had used hit my nostrils, and I vomited. Later I found out that the disinfectant was Cyclon A, a cousin of the poison gas Cyclon B. We got into our car, and we drove away as fast as we could. When we were a distance from the camp, we got out of the car, and poured water on our hands, the Jewish custom when we leave the cemetery. We drove as far as we could, until we reached the border of Czechoslovakia. Only then could we take out some food and eat, after fasting all day.

In Prague we found the Pinkas synagogue that my ancestors had built, and we saw the graves of famous rabbis from our family in the Jewish cemetery. It was a moving and restorative experience for all of us when the next day, on Shabbat, Uzi and the boys made the *minyan* in the oldest synagogue, in the Alt-Neu-Shul. There were no young people around, and they only had a few visitors those days, so they asked Jonathan to chant the *Haftarah,* the portion from the Prophets. On our way back, in Bratislava, we searched for and found the underground graves of some of the great rabbis who had lived in that part of Europe before the Holocaust. There we met an old Jew whom we first saw in Budapest, feeding birds crumbs from the community kitchen and whom we had named the "Bird Man." He could barely walk with his swollen legs, but he kept wandering through the camps and towns, still searching for his lost family.

The trip was very important to all of us. It took me a long time to digest what I had seen and experienced. I am sure that that was true for our sons as well. We said goodbye to Jonathan and Benjie in Vienna; they both went back to Israel to continue their studies, and we returned to America together with Michael.

In 1992 Uzi and I took a trip again to Eastern Europe, together with our friends Clarann and Irv Goldring. They wanted to go with us to see the places we came from and where I was imprisoned during the war. We repeated the visits to Hungary, Poland, and Czechoslovakia, but this time we were also able to go to Cop (Csap), Uzi's birthplace, and also to Uzhorod (Ungvar), the city where Uzi went to Yeshiva and to the Hebrew Gymnasium. These places were still under Communist Ukrainian rule at that time, and we could move around only with our official guide. Our visit was disappointing because they did not give us enough time to be there, but we did find Uzi's old home, his schools, and some neighbors who remembered his family. Again, we visited Auschwitz-Birkenau, because something was pulling us there—a need to cry, a need to get angry again. We felt strengthened by the presence of our friends, and we continued our trip to Prague to recover.

Many years have passed since those trips. Although I am still immersed in the Holocaust through books and movies, I don't think we will go back there again. Because of the outbreak of new anti-Semitism in Europe, I don't wish to go there even for a vacation. I am fortunate to be living in America, where I feel safe and accepted. My love for Israel has brought me to that country every year, and I will continue to support it in whatever way I can, even if I don't live there.

I never take for granted the gift of life, the miracle of my survival, and all the wonderful things in my life. I often remind myself not to waste my days on this earth. Although I catch myself wanting to see, hear, and experience everything, I know that what is important is to spend my hours and my days meaningfully, to give to others what I can, and enjoy the simple rewards that I may overlook if I am careless. I thank God for having kept me alive and for having reached this day.

$$\mathcal{S}$$

HISTORICAL NOTES

"It is now generally acknowledged that the Holocaust in Hungary represents the most controversial chapter in the history of the catastrophe that befell European Jewry during the Nazi era. It is a chapter replete with paradoxes. While the Jews in the other parts of Nazi-dominated Europe were being systematically destroyed, the Jews of Hungary were relatively well-off, enjoying the physical protection of the conservative-aristocratic regime. Although this regime was publicly committed to the 'solution' of the Jewish question, it abhorred the Nazis' ideologically defined Final Solution program as much as it hated—and feared—the Arrow Cross (*Nyilas*), the virulently anti-Semitic extremists who were dedicated to the building of a new national-socialist order in Hungary.

The Jews themselves, while suffering the consequences of increasingly harsh anti-Semitic measures, and incurring the loss of close to 60,000 lives by the end of 1943, implicitly trusted the conservative-aristocratic regime, convinced that it would continue to physically protect them. To the end they lived under the illusion that the Hungarians, appreciative of the Jews' loyalty and consistent support of the Magyar cause since 1848, would not allow them to suffer the tragic fate that had befallen their counterparts elsewhere in Nazi-dominated Europe. Their optimism was reinforced by the fact that Hungary, though an ally of Nazi Germany, was sovereign and independent, and that the Axis powers, given their military reversals since the end of 1942, were bound to lose the war. Like many of their conservative-aristocratic protectors, the Jews did not—and could not—anticipate the possibility that Nazi Germany would invade Hungary—a country whose location and economic and military support they deemed strategically important for the Axis cause.

But it was precisely because of these factors that Hitler was resolved to frustrate Hungary's intentions to extricate itself from the Axis Alliance by emulating Italy's successful example in the summer of 1943. Unlike Italy, however, Hungary was both overcautious and inept, paralyzed by the fear of a possible Soviet occupation. The conservative leadership took no precautionary measures against a possible German invasion, and continued to pursue fundamentally illusory objectives. Quixotically, the Hungarians were eager to surrender exclusively to the Western Powers, retain the antiquated social order together with the territories they had acquired between 1938 and 1941, and avoid at all cost any Soviet occupation. Clearly, they were more fearful of Bolshevism than Nazism, even if that entailed a German occupation. Hitler, aware of the Hungarians' machinations, decided to defend the interests of the Third Reich by occupying Hungary on March 19, 1944.

It was this military decision that sealed the fate of the approximately 825,000 Jews (including close to 100,000 converts and Christians identified as Jews under the anti-Jewish laws then in effect)—the last relatively intact Jewish community in Nazi-dominated Europe. It is one of the ironies of history that this community, having survived the first four and a half years of the war, was destroyed on the eve of the Allied victory when the secrets of Auschwitz were already widely known."

—Professor Randolph L. Braham, Director of the Rosenthal Institute for Holocaust Studies, City University of New York

(quoted with Prof. Braham's permission)

Erika's maternal grandparents, Joseph and Julia Salamonovics,
and their children and grandchildren, 1936, Edeleny.
Erika is sitting on the floor; next to her is her younger brother,
Moshu, her parents in the first row, right side.

Erika's paternal grandparents and their children, Hajdudorog, Hungary, 1930's
Zev Farkas Engel, Chana Engel, Yitzhak-gen, Shmilu-Lajos, Emma Gittel-Gizi

Erika, her parents
Jenö (Yakov Koppel) Engel
Malvina (Miriam) Salamonovics Engel
her brothers Tibor (Moshu) and Zoltan (Yitzchak)

Chicken plucking, Miskolc, 1940
L to r, Lilli, Marineni, Mari, Erika

Erika's graduation from the Jewish middle school, Miskolc, 1942

Erika, Miskolc, 1943

Erika with Religious Zionist Youth group six months after the liberation.
(She gained a lot of weight.)

Erika and Uzi's engagement
Budapest
November 29, 1947

Erika and her mother, Anyu
Havana Cuba, 1948

The first coat in New York after arriving from Cuba, winter, 1949

Erika and Uzi's wedding
Brooklyn, New York
September 24, 1950

Visit to Eastern Europe
Uzi, Erika, and sons
Miskolc, June, 1979

Erika's mother's 80th birthday
Top Row: Zoltan Engel (Erika's brother) and Uzi
Seated: Fruma Engel (Zoltan's wife), mother, Anyu, and Erika

Family Reunion
Canada, August, 1998

Family reunion
New York, February 23, 2000

Document issued in Peteswaldau, Germany, on May 28, 1945, to facilitate
Erika's return to Hungary after the liberation.

Document issued in Hungary registering Erika as a returning survivor
Budapest, June 13, 1945